THIRD EDITION

A VERY SHORT, FAIRLY INTERESTING AND REASONABLY CHEAP BOOK ABOUT STUDYING ORGANIZATIONS

CHRIS GREY

Los Angeles | London | New Delhi
Singapore | Washington DC

Los Angeles | London | New Delhi
Singapore | Washington DC

SAGE Publications Ltd
1 Oliver's Yard
55 City Road
London EC1Y 1SP

SAGE Publications Inc.
2455 Teller Road
Thousand Oaks, California 91320

SAGE Publications India Pvt Ltd
B 1/I 1 Mohan Cooperative Industrial Area
Mathura Road
New Delhi 110 044

SAGE Publications Asia-Pacific Pte Ltd
3 Church Street
#10-04 Samsung Hub
Singapore 049483

Editor: Kirsty Smy
Editorial assistant: Ruth Stitt
Production editor: Rachel Eley
Copyeditor: Jane Elliott
Proofreader: Sharon Cawood
Indexer: Avril Ehrlich
Marketing manager: Alison Borg
Cover design: Wendy Scott
Typeset by: C&M Digitals (P) Ltd, Chennai, India
Printed and bound by Henry Ling Limited,
at the Dorset Press, Dorchester, DT1 1HD

This title for the 'Very Short, Fairly Interesting and
Reasonably Cheap Book about…Series' was devised
by Chris Grey. His book, *A Very Short, Fairly Interesting
and Reasonably Cheap Book about Studying
Organizations*, was the founding title of this series.

Chris Grey asserts his rights to be recognized as
founding editor of the **Very Short, Fairly Interesting
and Reasonably Cheap Book about…Series**.

Library of Congress Control Number: 2012936380

British Library Cataloguing in Publication data

A catalogue record for this book is available from
the British Library

MIX
Paper from
responsible sources

FSC
www.fsc.org   **FSC® C013985**

ISBN 978-1-4462-0736-9
ISBN 978-1-4462-0737-6 (pbk)

Also in this series:

Brad Jackson and Ken Parry, *A Very Short, Fairly Interesting and Reasonably Cheap Book about Studying Leadership*, 2nd edition

Chris Carter, Stewart Clegg and Martin Kornberger, *A Very Short, Fairly Interesting and Reasonably Cheap Book about Studying Strategy*

Ann L. Cunliffe, *A Very Short, Fairly Interesting and Reasonably Cheap Book about Management*

Bob Garvey, *A Very Short, Fairly Interesting and Reasonably Cheap Book about Coaching and Mentoring*

George Cairns and Martyna Sliwa, *A Very Short, Fairly Interesting and Reasonably Cheap Book about International Business*

Jim Blythe, *A Very Short, Fairly Interesting and Reasonably Cheap Book about Studying Marketing*

Dedicated to Alan Grey (1926–2005)

Contents

About the Author

Chris Grey is Professor of Organization Studies at the School of Management at Royal Holloway, University of London. Before that he held Professorships at the Universities of Warwick and Cambridge. He is also Visiting Research Fellow at Cambridge and has been Velux Foundation Visiting Professor at Copenhagen Business School, Denmark, Visiting Professor at the Université Paris-Dauphine, France and a Visiting Fellow at the Stockholm Centre for Organizational Research, Sweden. Between 2010 and 2012 he was a Leverhulme Major Research Fellow. For six years he was Editor-in-Chief of *Management Learning* and is currently an Associate Editor of *Organization* and a European Co-editor of the *Journal of Management Inquiry*. Apart from publishing numerous articles in academic journals, he co-edited *Rethinking Management Education* (Sage, 1996), *Essential Readings in Management Learning* (Sage, 2004) and *Critical Management Studies: A Reader* (Oxford University Press, 2005), co-authored *Making Up Accountants* (Gower Ashgate, 1998) and is the author of *Decoding Organization: Bletchley Park, Codebreaking and Organization Studies* (Cambridge University Press, 2012). He currently has an eclectic mix of research interests, including the organization of intelligence and security agencies, but his real passion is detective novels and he will one day write the definitive contribution to that genre. He was born in Croydon (Britain's 'New Manhattan'!) in 1964 and may very well be one of the leading organizational theorists that town has produced.

Acknowledgements
to the Third Edition

I continue to be grateful to all those acknowledged in the first and second editions. Amongst those Madeleine Grey, Nathalie Mitev Grey and Andrew Sturdy in particular have continued to be enormously supportive, both personally and intellectually, of what I have tried to achieve in developing this book further. At Sage I am grateful to my former editors Kiren Shoman and Natalie Aguilera, my present editor Kirsty Smy and her former assistant Ruth Stitt. I also appreciate very much the work of five anonymous reviewers commissioned by Sage to comment on the second edition in order to advise on the development of this third edition. Much of the new edition was prepared whilst I was Velux Foundation Visiting Professor at the Department of Organization, Copenhagen Business School (CBS), Denmark, as part of the 'What Makes Organization (WMO)?' research programme. I am extremely grateful to Paul du Gay for inviting me there, for his great kindness during my visit and for the many fascinating conversations I had with him. Amongst many others at CBS, I am grateful to Karen Boll, Dan Kärreman, Kristian Kreiner, Maria Lundberg and Signe Vikkelsø for providing a supportive environment and some invigorating conversations during my visit. A parallel visit to the Department of Business Administration at Lund University, Sweden provided similarly inspiring conversations, in particular with Mats Alvesson. I owe a particular debt to Marie Mathiesen and Susanne Ekman at CBS, not only for their own considerable contribution to making me feel welcome there but also for making detailed and incredibly useful comments on much of the new material in this edition. It goes without saying that none of those named bears any responsibility for any errors of fact or interpretation in this book.

Chris Grey

Should You Buy this Book?

This book is mainly designed for university students who are studying organizations, probably as part of a management course, whether undergraduate or postgraduate. It is not a textbook, and assumes some knowledge of the field. It's also for people who aren't on one of these courses but are interested in organizations and management, perhaps because of their experience of these. And it might also be for academics working in the field who would like to read an overview of a less conventional approach.

You should buy this book if:

- you're bored by the obese textbook your lecturer has recommended
- you've got the feeling that the textbook stuff is a bit dubious
- you've found that the recommended 'extra reading' is boring
- you'd like to read something stimulating, but not too turgid and worthy
- you'd like to show your lecturer you've done some extra reading
- you want a different take on organizations and management
- you don't want to spend too much money.

You should not buy this book if:

- you want a textbook
- you want bullet points (these are almost the last ones), boxes of text, further reading, further questions and all the usual patronizing stuff
- you're happy to get a minimal pass out of the textbook
- you don't want to have some of your ideas challenged
- you're not too bright at the end of the day
- you want heroic stories about great leaders, fantastic companies and how all is right with the world
- you haven't got even the modest price of the book, or have better things to do with it.

If you do buy this book and want to come back on anything in it, you can email me at: chris.grey@sagepub.co.uk. You can also follow my blog relating to this book at http://author-chrisgrey.blogspot.co.uk.

Preface to the Third Edition

When I wrote the original version of this book, I never imagined or expected that there would be further editions of it and yet I now find myself preparing a third edition. In fact, when the idea of a second edition was raised by Kiren Shoman, then my editor at Sage, it was one which I initially resisted. New editions of textbooks are common, as authors seek to keep references and topics up to date. But this isn't a textbook, and in some ways doesn't need updating in that it is a particular *argument* about the study of organizations and, whatever its failings, this argument isn't really time specific.

Nevertheless, there was a second edition, and now there is a third. In fact I have had fewer reservations about this third one than I did about the second. Because there is a story to be told which may be interesting – at least 'reasonably interesting' – about how this book has developed and the reactions to it. I have been both surprised and gratified by how much interest the book has generated, and I want to reflect upon that, not (or not only, anyway) for reasons of self-aggrandizement but because I think it discloses something of significance about the current state of academic work in the field of organization studies. Most of this preface will be devoted to that. But the other reason is that in developing the second edition I added in quite a bit of new material about the financial crisis that broke around the time I was preparing it; and this material does indeed need updating in the conventional sense of paying attention to events which have unfolded since. This has actually proved to be a rather bitter-sweet experience since the second edition read, in parts, almost prophetically about what was likely to happen. But since as part of the update I can hardly continually say 'I told you so', it seems that perhaps the only time in my life when I have made accurate predictions about the future must now disappear from view. So those reading this new edition will just have to take it on trust, or else hunt down the previous edition to check for themselves, that I did, indeed, tell you so.

Most of that updating occurs in Chapter 5, which is almost completely new, and to a lesser extent in Chapters 3 and 4. One consequence of trying to include material on current events which are developing rapidly is that it almost immediately becomes dated again. So I should mention here, as I do again at various points in the text, that my account of these events was finalized in March 2012. Despite this limitation, recent and current events have made me more certain than ever that the study of organizations must speak of and to financial, economic and political domains. An altogether different kind of updating has taken place with respect to Chapter 6. Indeed careful readers will observe that there is no Chapter 6, because the updating has taken the form of removing this chapter, which was mainly about the business school context within which the study of organizations mostly takes place. A few parts of this material have been redeployed elsewhere in the book, but most of it has now gone. The main reason for this was simply to remain true to the original idea of keeping the book 'very short' – the second edition having been considerably longer than the first, and the third edition threatening to become even more so. It is with some regret that I made this excision, both because I think this business school context is important and because I know from feedback that many readers found it interesting. However, it was at least partly tangential to the main lines of argument and since something had to go, this was where the axe fell. Those who wish to read it can access it at http://www.uk.sagepub.com/grey.

The biggest challenge in developing the second and now, even more, the third edition has been that the first edition had a very particular tone and style which is impossible to recapture. Some readers have said that reading the book feels like a conversation but it is inevitable that, over the course of the now nine years since I wrote the original version, the way I 'talk' has changed. I haven't attempted to unify the style except in the sense that it remains fairly conversational, and I am sure that the joins show in places as a result. Actually, for me the biggest problem has not been trying to write now as I wrote before, but the fact that parts of what I wrote before now make me cringe, rather in the way that seeing an old photograph of yourself in what now seem embarrassing clothes and with an embarrassing haircut makes you cringe. But since many readers have been kind enough to say that they liked that style, it would seem perverse to expunge it. So all I have done in that regard is to remove some of the phrases and expressions which I now find too shame-making.

Let me now talk about reactions to the book, and as a prelude I would like to say something about what I originally hoped to achieve with it. I felt that there was a space for something which was neither textbook nor research monograph, and which communicated, to students in particular, something about the gap between what is presented as established knowledge in the former and the way that that knowledge is very often problematized in the latter. I actually had some wider aspirations, too, which the book only partially realized. I hoped that it might be possible to reach an audience beyond students and academics; to appeal to that most elusive of creatures, the 'general reader'.

Perhaps because the book contained an email address and an invitation to make comments, I have had a great deal of feedback from readers – far more than I've received about anything else I've written. Some of this reaction is reproduced on the cover, and it is not just the usual marketing blurb in that probably 99 per cent of the correspondents were positive and a few even said that the book had changed their lives, so the quotes on the cover were actually selected from a much larger number of similar comments. A few of those who wrote took me to task for some of the arguments but only one – a student in New Zealand who I will not name, but who may well speak for many who did not choose to write to me – was entirely negative, telling me that the book was irredeemably dull and worthless and inviting me never to write a word again. Charming as her email was, it will be obvious that I have declined her invitation. I was particularly pleased to receive several complimentary emails from people who were indeed general readers and for whom the main attraction was that the book provided an anti-dote to the otherwise ubiquitous managerialism to which they were exposed in their working lives.

Whilst this reaction has been gratifying, it has come largely from an audience I hoped to address. What has been more striking is the way that the book has attracted the attention of the scholarly community and also of journalists. Amongst the latter, Simon Caulkin of the *Observer* and Stefan Stern of the *Financial Times* both wrote appreciative articles around the book. In the academic literature, there have been reviews in many journals treating the book not simply as a primer for students, but also as containing a serious argument about the nature of the organiza-tion theory discipline. Those reviews have been broadly positive – as is inevitable with a book of this sort, some have profoundly disagreed with my fundamental position, a view I can respect whilst of course not sharing. There have also been predictably – and, in fact, predicted in the book – waspish attacks on my attempt at accessibility (for some, perversely one might have thought, the ultimate accolade for a writer is to be unreadable and unread). It is a very considerable temptation to reply to some of these reviews here, at least the negative ones, but perhaps it would be 'unrea-sonably cheap' to do so. All that I would say on this point is that the most negative reactions seem to have come from those within the 'critical management studies' community, rather than from what one might call the mainstream. That is perhaps curious and depressing since what is contained in this book is some version of critical management studies (CMS). What it reflects, I suppose, is what has been the traditional ten-dency of the political Left (and CMS is to a large extent a version of Leftism) to prize 'purism' and punish perceived 'betrayals'.

I would, however, like to pick up on a comment made within the very supportive and generous review from the leading Finnish organizational theorist Janne Tienari (2006). He made the point that many of the examples I use are British, and so parochial. I think that he is right, and I don't think that this third edition is any great improvement on the first in that respect. My only defences are the trivial one that I happen to be British; and the more important one, made again in Chapter 5, that the British case is revealing to the extent that, having been the 'first industrial nation', Britain is also a testing ground for many of the innovations and ideologies of the 'new capitalism'. It is still the case, for example, that the politics of former British Prime Minister Margaret Thatcher are invoked in many countries during discussions of how economic 'reform' should (or should not) proceed. But I do acknowledge the problem, and apologise for my failure really to address it in this new edition, except to the extent that the global nature of the financial crisis has enabled me to refer, again mainly in Chapter 5, to the economic experiences of a variety of countries.

The scale of the reactions, and the diversity of audiences from which they have come, and the very strong sales it has enjoyed, suggest to me that, despite the flaws and shortcomings the book most certainly has, it has been successful in being seen as 'a different kind of book'. It is difficult to think of many books about organizations which have garnered reaction – still less largely positive reaction – from students, academics, journalists and general readers alike. The reason may be worth reflecting upon.

The world of organizations and the way we make sense of them is immensely important because it is central to many, perhaps most, people's lives. But it has been almost entirely evacuated by academics and intellectuals who have any apparent desire to communicate. There are certainly exceptions to this[1] (e.g. Parker, 2002; Ehrenreich, 2006; Sennett, 2006; Aubenas, 2011; Standing, 2011), but from most of us whose job it is to explore organizational life there is little to be heard outside of the stunted and stultifying world of academic journals. One reason for this is the way that most organization studies takes place in business schools. This, at least in most 'elite' schools, is a largely sterile atmosphere in which to do work that does not simply reproduce managerial orthodoxy. The general tendency in such institutions is to an ever-more slavish conformity to league tables and rankings (of schools, programmes, journals, etc.) which make the possibility of any kind of serious intellectual work, and certainly the expression of heterodox opinion, increasingly rare and difficult. On the other hand, outside of the 'elite' business schools it is certainly possible – indeed relatively easy – to produce work on organizations which is more intellectually engaged and more unorthodox.

There are many such schools, especially in the UK, Scandinavia, Australia and New Zealand. And within those schools there are many highly gifted and critically-minded scholars. Yet, despite the existence of this latter group, the business school world is a peculiar one in which the MBA audience, in particular, is by and large exposed to trivialities whilst the academics get on with – well, what? It's a complicated story, in two parts.

The first part is to do with the journals, publication in which is what makes academics' careers. In conventional eyes, these fall roughly into three tiers. The first tier is the North American 'elite' journals, associated with the 'elite' business schools. These offer little prospect of interesting writing, being largely the preserve of abstract, supposedly scientific, quantitative analysis; or of qualitative analysis but written in similarly abstract and technicist ways. Then there is a second tier which is mainly European. In the 1980s and 1990s these journals often carried very interesting work, and some of it is referred to in this book. But in recent years they have to a large extent become obsessed with being recognized by the 'first tier', and as a result most of their articles are dull, formulaic and unchallenging (see Grey, 2010 for more on this). Then there is the third tier, which is a huge proliferation of specialized journals of very variable quality which allow just about anything to be published: some of it far, far better than anything found in the 'higher tier' journals, by virtue of being freed from their constraints; some of it simply dross, sharing all the defects of the 'better' journals whilst lacking even the patina of professional competence that those journals demand. Readers who are not academics need to understand two things about the world of academic journal publishing. One is that it interests most academics far more than anything else because, not necessarily unreasonably, it is what makes or breaks our reputations. The other is that the content of these journals, of whatever tier, is neither read by nor – by and large – of interest to anyone outside the academic community, and even then only to segments of it. My criticisms here should not be confused with the relentless call for 'relevance' to which research on organizations and management is constantly, and increasingly, exposed. Those calls inevitably construe 'relevance' as 'relevance to corporate and managerial interests'. My concern is rather with the need to make our work relevant and accessible to a wide range of people with a plurality of interests. And I can say this without, I hope, being accused of ignorance or of sour grapes – although perhaps of hypocrisy – because I have spent much of my working life publishing in academic journals.

Then there is a second part to the reason why organization studies speaks to very few people. It is not just the stultifying impact of business schools or the conservatism of major journals. The intellectually oriented and politically progressive members of the organization studies academic community have increasingly become sunk into obscurantism. Every year a tidal wave of writing is produced about this or that theorist – Lacan, Žižek, Deleuze are current favourites, although the real avant-garde no doubt consider these old hat. The writing style tends to be pretentious and smug; for all the talk of 'reflexivity', the authors rarely offer their own views but simply parade the views of the great theorists before whom they bow down in ritualistic obeisance. This is neither to criticize 'theoretical' writing per se nor to deny the very substantial value of the introduction of a broad swathe of thinkers from other social sciences or philosophy by many pioneers in organization studies, to whom this book is substantially indebted. Rather it is to deplore the recent tendency to do so in ways which obscure rather than illuminate (see Grey and Sinclair, 2006).

So it is within this rather unsatisfactory context that I understand the reactions to the first edition of this book. The establishment is largely moribund (as establishments must necessarily be); what used to be the challengers to the establishment have, not entirely but largely, been incorporated to the extent of being almost equally dull and trivial; the new challengers are too often obscure and pretentious. I said earlier that I didn't want to be self-aggrandizing in speaking of the positive reactions to this book. Having set out the context to these reactions it will be clear that, far from being self-aggrandizing, the main reason why the book was well-received is the parlous state of the field. On the one hand, we have a topic of importance to huge numbers of people, and the subject of study for a considerable section of the student population; on the other hand, we have a group of academics whose job it is to speak about this topic and to these people, but who – for various reasons – signally fail to do so. For within all of this writing, of whatever school or camp, you would be hard-pressed to find much which seems to have any great connection – sometimes any connection at all – with the experience of work.

Let me be clear that it is not my intention to give aid and succour to anti-intellectualism. In the book I make much use of the notion of unintended consequences, and one of the unintended consequences of its reception has been that a few have seen it – usually as misplaced criticism, occasionally as misplaced praise – as giving license to people to avoid difficult or complex ideas (apparently not recognizing that the book itself would have been impossible without the prior existence of a difficult and complex literature; and in a sense the book is an attempt to translate that literature into a more comprehensible form). So to clarify: I certainly don't think that students need do no more than read this little book to have an adequate grasp of the field; I certainly don't think that the way that I have written it is the only worthwhile way to write; and I certainly don't intend my criticism of critical writing in the field to validate bluff, commonsense empiricism or dismissive small-mindedness.

Nor has this been the only unintended consequence. I originally intended this book to be in some way an alternative – an alternative to the academic literature and to the textbooks – which might, I hoped, appeal to students precisely because it tried to connect to and to articulate what might be their own reservations about existing writings. But as it has turned out, it has been used in many places as the 'official text'. Indeed in some places students are assessed on its contents as if it were some kind of repository of authorized knowledge. For such students, the book can hardly be seen as 'alternative'. I'm obviously not complaining about this – I'm actually rather flattered, I suppose – and it would make no difference even if I did. But it is an irony of which I am all too well aware.

The other ironic and unintended consequence is that the book has now spawned a whole series of 'very short, fairly interesting and reasonably cheap' books about this, that and the other. It has become a 'brand'. This development was one which, like the writing of new editions, I initially resisted and the story behind it is strange. When I originally proposed the title, it caused some questions to be raised as it did not fit established categories of marketing. To the credit of my then editor, Kiren Shoman, and to Sage more generally, the title was eventually accepted. But I certainly did not envisage it becoming the brand of a series and, although of course I wish my fellow authors well and admire them for what they have done with the format, I remain slightly bemused by the way it has developed as such.

However, whatever unintended consequences have flowed from the book's publication, the guiding spirit of this third edition remains as it was from the outset: to contribute to the project of critique, at the heart of which is a politics of transformation and emancipation. And to convey my sense, angry but still optimistic, that such a politics is possible. This politics ultimately calls for a re-evaluation of dominant ideologies associated with unrestrained capitalism, instrumental rationality and managerialism. We are living through some dramatic events, but to say so does not imply the detached voice of an observer because it is a time of much suffering. And within that suffering there is much which relates to the study of organizations: unemployment, under-employment, the erosion of welfare, the ever-more intrusive and stringent demands made of those who are in work, the growing insecurity of the old and the destruction of hope amongst the young, and the increasing sense of interlinked crises in global finance, economics and politics. But what does mainstream organization studies have to say about these things? Virtually nothing. So I continue to hope that, despite its having been in some ways institutionalized and commodified, this book still has for some readers the capacity to offer a different kind of way of talking, writing and thinking about organizations.

 note

1 It is noteworthy, given what I am about to say about academic journals, that the examples I have given are all books (and that three of the authors are journalists). Books do offer a greater possibility for communicative writing but even here the kind of communication I am arguing for is rare, and the textbook and monograph pre-dominate the genre. One reason may be that popular books about management are such a degraded form (i.e. of the general sort *Zap! Ten Ways to Transform Your Business*). But the space surely exists for books – perhaps in the mode of the work of some historians – which are accessible without being unbearably trite?

Introduction: Why Studying Organizations Matters to Me

The chief object of education is not to learn things but to unlearn things.

G.K. Chesterton

The purpose of this short book is to say some things about the study of organizations which seem to me to be true. In putting it that way, I am signalling that this is not a textbook, not just because it is far shorter than a textbook but because it has no pretensions to comprehensiveness, and I'm going to assume you've read a textbook or that you have some familiarity with ideas about organizations. Nor is it a specific contribution to scholarship advancing a novel or narrowly defined thesis. Indeed, it is scarcely original at all, except in the sense that the particular things I exclude and the way I put together what I do include are specific to this book. But that kind of originality may be as much a defect as a virtue.

It is, as I say, a short book, and that is for a reason other than laziness or ignorance on my part. The field of management studies, which is where most of the study of organizations occurs, is increasingly characterized by huge, door-stopping, wrist-aching textbooks running sometimes to many hundreds of pages, and also by a proliferation of readers, handbooks and treatises. Whatever merits they may have, they certainly have some serious disadvantages including the physical strain of carrying and reading them. The most obvious is that, in my experience, people don't actually read them – at least not in their entirety. They are also expensive, sometimes prohibitively so. I wanted to create a book that would fit in the average sized pocket, and not burn a hole in that pocket; a book which could be carried and read on a single longish train or plane journey, say. And I wondered if one way of achieving that was to write in a slightly different way to that which is the norm amongst academics.

Which brings me to my second motivation. Instead of writing a long, comprehensive, scholarly or original book, I have tried to write an interesting book about studying organizations – in many ways a more difficult task. Why is it worth undertaking? After all, is there really a need for yet another book on organizations? There are so many already, whether they bear the weighty burden of declaiming the subjects of organizational behaviour, theory and analysis[1]; the advancement of a provocative new angle; or the populist desire to transform the thinking of travelling executives. How many of these are interesting, though, is another question. Many include material which is palpably false. Others announce the blindingly obvious. Still others specialize in the accidentally or wilfully obscure. And all three of these types conspire to be, with a few honourable exceptions, very, very dull.

And yet I passionately believe that organizations are incredibly interesting. In one way, to study them is to study just about every facet of human life. It's true that most of the study of organizations has been concerned with the corporations and institutions where people work, and usually the larger ones at that. But more fundamentally, all forms of collective activity – politics, the family, as well as work – are about organization in some way. Which also means – and it's a major failing of most books to ignore this – that to study organizations involves thinking about philosophy, politics, ethics and much more. And behind or beyond these abstractions are the lived experiences of people not just working together but joking, arguing, criticizing, fighting, deciding, lusting, despairing, creating, resisting, fearing, hoping or, in short, organizing. I don't find it easy to imagine a world without organizations, but I also don't find it easy to recognize that world in the mainstream books about organizations.

If this is so then organization theory – the study of organizations – must also be important. In this book I will talk about both organizations and organization theory because these are so closely related. The way we think about organizations – even to the extent of what we recognize as being an organization – is inseparable from some kind of organization theory. And organization theory has often been used not just to 'think about' but to act within and upon organizations, so that they bear its imprint. So I don't think it is helpful to draw too much of a line between the two and, except where it is important to do otherwise, I won't try to do so.

A more difficult distinction is that between organization theory and organizations, on the one hand, and management on the other. This is partly because management is, in most cases, an interesting and important part of organizational life and therefore of the study of organizational life. It is also partly because, as I have already mentioned, most organization theory is nowadays conducted as part of management studies. Relatedly, it is because much organization theory treats organizations solely or primarily from the point of view of how to manage them (better) – how to get the job done. For that reason, each chapter of this book discusses an aspect of the study of organizations but links this to an aspect of management.

I will say a great deal about this linkage between organization theory and management in this book, but for now I will just point out that when organizations are simply thought about in terms of 'getting the job done', it cuts out so much that matters – who says what the job is, who says how it should be done and how are people affected by getting it done this rather than that way? I think that these are really important issues and this book is animated in part by an anger that they are almost entirely ignored by the bulk of organization theory and the huge number of courses in business and management which are offered by universities. But I also think, with less anger but with a degree of sadness, that those people within organization theory who have raised the issues with which this book is concerned have often done so in a way which is inaccessible to all but a tiny fraction of the population. I am not pointing the finger in saying this, because I have done the same thing. But in this book I want to rectify this by communicating something of the more critical[2] orientations of organization theory in a way that those who would not otherwise be aware of them can, without too much difficulty, understand.

It should be easy to write an interesting book about organizations, and difficult to write a boring one. I haven't found it to be so and, most likely, haven't succeeded in doing so. This book has taken a long time to write, even though I've been thinking about it for ages. One reason – maybe an idiosyncratic one – is that every time I tried to write something interesting, I felt, as if it were at my shoulder, a hypothetical reviewer criticizing: 'the argument is confused'; 'the author seems unaware of Joe Blogg's groundbreaking paper from last year'; 'the author misunderstands Josephine Blogg's seminal book'; 'theoretically naïve'; 'lacking evidence'; or, worst of all, 'Grey hasn't got a clue – as we have long suspected'.

To placate this imagined reader (who may well have been me), I kept trying, so far as I was able, to refine arguments, close gaps, add references, make qualifications, avoid sweeping assertions. I sought the comments of colleagues, and tried to incorporate them. I worried more about what I didn't know than what I did. In short, I tried to be more comprehensive and more scholarly. So the book got longer and longer, and it was taking longer and longer to write (I'm talking years), which meant that I had to keep reading new material being published. The bibliography took on a nasty, spiteful life of its own. I felt more and more bored by the whole thing. And reasoning that if even I felt bored by it then most readers would surely feel even more so, I threw the manuscript in the bin (today – at the very moment I wrote these words). It's true that it lurks somewhere on my computer – partly as a terrible warning, partly because I might at some point want to write a book that bores me – but I felt the urge to try something different. This is it.

a different kind of book

Imagine a world where the thing which dominated it (God, the Party, Parliament – whatever you want) was written about in one of three ways. One was like a Bible: very heavy and entirely orthodox. The second was amusing and readable but didn't begin to tell you anything you couldn't think for yourself, and never once suggested that the Bible was wrong. The third seemed to say some things you wouldn't think yourself, and suggested flaws in the Bible, but you couldn't understand it because it was so obscurely written.

In that imaginary world you might well feel dissatisfied. In this real world, the thing that permeates just about everything is organizations and their management. You are born in a hospital; you go to school or university; you belong to, say, a sports club or a church; you go to work. You deal with – what? – supermarkets, banks, mobile phone companies – whatever.

And if you want to understand these things – or, maybe, if you have to because you are doing a management course – then you have pretty much the same three choices as in the imaginary world of the previous paragraph. The textbook that gives you the authorized orthodoxy; the pop management book that you understand but which states the patently obvious and is no more than a better written version of the orthodoxy; or the scholarly book that may challenge the orthodoxy but which is mainly unreadable.

So maybe there is a space for a different kind of book. This is an attempt at it. What I want to capture is something which sometimes comes to me when I am teaching my undergraduate students. They typically know relatively little about the literature on organizations and what they do know they have some scepticism about. But they are intelligent, well-educated and curious. So in class discussions I find myself, on good days, talking with a degree of passion but with relatively little regard for 'the literature', for a 'consistent' theoretical position or for the reviewer on my shoulder. And at least some of my students seem to appreciate that, which makes me wonder if a wider audience, mainly of students but hopefully of others, might also be interested. This book doesn't quite capture those classroom discussions – writing and reading are, after all, different media to talking – but it is written in that spirit. I have given myself the freedom to try to communicate, rather than to obscure. In some respects, the aspiration to write an interesting book raises higher expectations than those incited by a comprehensive or scholarly one. As I have said, I doubt whether I have succeeded, but I have found it more enjoyable than not to have tried. To my scholarly colleagues I offer an apology for the superficiality and violence with which I have treated their ideas, but make a suggestion I will return to: sophistication is sometimes bought at a price which is not worth paying.

people who study organizations

Trying to write an interesting book is one thing, but, going back to the first sentence of this introduction, another set of issues obtrudes. I said that I wanted to write some things about the study of organizations which seem to me to be true. That, I think, will be a perfectly intelligible goal to most readers. It may seem a peculiar or even eccentric goal – why don't I just do some DIY or go to the pub like everyone else? – but, given that eccentricity, at least it makes sense. Yet, curiously and perhaps worryingly, this very first sentence will raise the hackles of just about all of my colleagues whose academic profession is the study of organizations. I think it's worth saying something about this, partly for them but mainly because, for others, it may clarify the purpose, and difficulty, of this book.

Organization theorists – the people who study organizations for a living – come in all kinds of hues. They adhere to a multiplicity of schools of thought which they defend and aggress with remarkable passion. But there are some quite fundamental camps into which many, or most, fall. One distinction is between those who believe that organization theory is, or will become, a science not unlike the natural sciences. It's a loose term, but that view can be described as 'positivism'. Maybe the core of positivism is that there exists an observable, objective organizational reality which exists independent of organization theory. The task of organization theory is to uncover this reality and discover the laws by which it operates, and perhaps then to predict future events. They tend to favour quantitative research. Then there is a second camp, which denies this scientific view. They might be called 'interpretivists' or 'constructivists' or 'relativists', and in their view (or views, for these are not quite identical terms) organizational reality does not have an objective existence but is constructed by people in organizations and by organization theory itself. There are no laws to be discovered and prediction is well-nigh impossible. They tend to favour qualitative work.

One simple way to think of this distinction is to imagine a cricket umpire making an LBW (leg before wicket) decision (or a football referee judging an off-side, if you prefer). The 'positivist' view would be that it either is an LBW or it isn't, and the umpire either gets it right or wrong. The 'constructivist' view would be that if it's called as LBW then it is LBW. One appeals to an objective fact (what the ball did) and the other to a social fact (how it was interpreted by people, especially powerful people). Actually, the constructivist might go further, and say that the rules about what counts as LBW are socially made anyway and so could be, and sometimes are, changed. Note that either of these views can be called 'realistic', the first because it is about what *really* happened with ball, leg and wicket; the second because it is about what *really* happened in terms of the batsman being given out and being back in the pavilion. They are 'just' different versions of what can be meant by reality. (Amusingly, my cricket-challenged but social theory-knowledgeable wife is the only person to whom I have used this example in reverse in order to explain what LBW means.)

As this book goes on I will touch again on these debates but for now I want to point out that, from both of these positions, the aspiration to 'say some things about the study of organizations which seem to me to be true' looks distinctly dodgy. For the positivists, the problem is the 'seem to me' part. 'Why should we be interested in Grey's subjective ramblings?' they will complain. 'What we want are the facts of the matter, as established by research.' For the constructivists, it's the 'true' part that is a worry. For them, there is perhaps only interpretation, and to dress this up as truth is an unbearable conceit.

My own sympathies are more with the latter (interpretivist, constructivist) view than with the former, and that is why the truth I am claiming to represent is of the 'seems to me' variety. But I will say to my positivist colleagues and readers who share their concerns that this book is a little bit more than subjective ramblings: it is, or aspires to be, an *argument* made up from fragments of the arguments of others and, if successful, articulated in a way which is plausible to the reader. And maybe that will assuage the constructivists a little, because it means that the truths I am so presumptuously offering are only staking a claim to plausibility, not to objective reality. To the positivists I want to say that the confidence with which they speak their truths is only achieved at the cost of an indefensible philosophical naïvety. But to the constructivists I want to say that the ultimate difficulty with their position is that they can become scared of saying anything at all (not that there is much sign of that) for fear of appearing philosophically naïve. In that case, we might as well all pack up and go home, which might save some paper but would be a shame given the enduring and endemic experience of organization in this and other societies.

There are other kinds of distinctions amongst those who study organizations. I've glossed the positivists as numerically-inclined scientists and the constructivists as description-inclined interpreters (and glossed is the right word). But another distinction which hazily and paradoxically links to this is that between managerialists and critics. The managerialists are interested in organizations from a particular point of view: that of how to manage them more effectively. This also implies that they share the interests, both political (whose side they take) and intellectual (what is analytically important to them), of managers. There is quite a bit of variety here, but these same people are very often the positivists. It isn't hard to see the linkage, for the goal of providing fact-based, reliable organizational predictions would, if realized, be very useful to managers. The paradox, of course, is that the traditional model of science has it as a value-neutral rather than a politically partisan enterprise.

The critics are more concerned with an understanding of the organization as a whole, with some partisan preference for the managed rather than the managers. And these critics are more commonly to be found in the constructivist camp. Because they do not hold out the hope of organizational predictions and control they tend to be seen as less useful to managers. In any case, they are much more likely to question, in all kinds of ways, the organizational status quo. This also means that, because the bulk of organization theory is currently done in management schools, the critics are considerably more marginal than the managerialists. The paradox is also present, in a rather more muted form, for in moving away from the values of management, the critics provide something more like, not a value-free account, but an analytical account of organizations.

Beyond the paradoxes there is an irony. The managerialist-positivist camp, for all their desire to speak effectively to the world of practice, have consistently failed to come up with anything of much use to managers or others, a fact for which they are consistently criticized and over which they themselves persistently agonize. Whereas the constructivist critics at least provide an account which is recognizably about actual people in organizations, rather than the abstract statistical hypothesis testing of their more mainstream colleagues.[3]

Within this axis, I position myself much more as a critic than a managerialist. There are all kinds of reasons for this, which I guess in the end just come down to politics. I don't particularly want to side with the relatively more powerful and I'm sceptical about the benefits of management in the ways that that activity is usually conducted. I think there is much more to organizations than the managerialists typically recognize and, indeed, that the conventional ways of managing organizations represent just one way in which organization could be conducted. In this sense I am, to borrow the words of Martin Parker (2002), 'against management' but 'for organization'.

Throughout this book, I will be conducting a kind of ongoing conversation across managerial and critical approaches. Sometimes I will be explaining one or other approach, but more often I will be trying to juxtapose them. Indeed, and this I know introduces some complex problems of exposition, in this conversation I am really using organization theory in two quite different ways. On the one hand, I will be talking about organization theory as a body of thinking espoused in mainstream and textbook accounts, usually of a managerialist kind. On the other hand, I will be using concepts from critically orientated organization theory to illuminate and challenge the conventional wisdom. Hopefully it will be clear at each point what meaning of organization theory I intend, but in any case this problem is an unavoidable result of the fissured character of organization theory. Of course I could just do what most writers do, which is to ignore those fissures and simply write from within one or other camp. But that would defeat my primary purpose, which is to provide for students with a mainly mainstream knowledge of organization theory a mainly critical commentary upon that knowledge. Many others have provided expositions of the mainstream, managerialist approach – almost all textbooks being examples. A few have outlined the critical approach. But because they tend to ignore each other, the former do not challenge established wisdom whilst the latter are too far removed from what non-specialist readers already know.

All of this self-positioning is meant to introduce those who are not already aware of it to some of the ways in which organization theory is a schismatic field in which every word used betrays an allegiance to this or that view. Organization theory is itself organized, and it is impossible to write about it without treading on someone's toes. The broad-brush account I have given of its schisms will have done just that for those initiated into these debates. But I would rather make broad, committed (and perhaps occasionally foolish) statements than become paralysed to unreadability by qualifications and elucidations. I think the *impasse* that organization theory has reached is that those with sophisticated understandings of organizations can only write for each other, whilst those who can write for broader audiences have only the most banal things to say.

To those of my colleagues who may blanch at the liberties I have taken with the ideas that they, and elsewhere I, propound in complex and elaborate terms in – oh, woeful phrase – 'the literature', I say two things. One is that, unfortunately for us, and perhaps for them, almost no one reads the literature. The other, more controversial thing is this: the demand for purity and sophistication is not always a noble defence of rigorous standards, it is sometimes a psychological defence which allows a feeling of superiority over others. It is easy and comforting to see one's own ideas as so sophisticated that any attempt at making them intelligible is to diminish them (and so oneself). However, given that organizations are such a pervasive and important feature of life it seems perverse to me that the most important contributions to organization theory can only be understood by a few hundred people in the world – if that many. I sometimes find myself at academic conferences and have the experience of simply not understanding what is being said. If that is true of someone who has spent some twenty-five years working in the field, who has contributed a fair amount to its literature and – modesty aside – is not a complete idiot, then something is wrong. Wrong with me, perhaps, for not understanding what is said; but as I have got older I have begun to acquire the self-confidence to believe that there may be something wrong with those doing the saying, or at least the way that they say it.

So my intention in this book is to try to say some fairly sophisticated things in a way which is fairly simply expressed. Of course these things are relative: and I am aware that, despite my best efforts, for some this will still seem like a heavy read. There is a certain point beyond which it is impossible to simplify without ceasing to say anything that isn't banal. But I've tried to write in an informal and conversational tone although I have avoided those textual devices – lists of bullet points, key concepts, text boxes – which, whilst beloved by publishers for their supposed accessibility, I always find patronizing, infantilizing and not even helpful. I've tried to write in a way that demands intelligence, but isn't pompous or patronizing, so those who object on the grounds that it is either too demanding or insufficiently weighty might with great wisdom choose to put it back on the bookshelves right now.

For those who continue with it, I hope this book will leaven the rather stodgy dough of, in particular, the textbooks, and it could be read as an accompaniment to many of these. I have deliberately framed much of the discussion around topics and authors which form the staple of textbooks, rather than introduce some of the more abstruse or obscure theorists (though there's a bit of that) because I want to take some rather tired old material with which students are already to some degree familiar, and comment upon it in ways which hopefully will be a bit fresher. But, to repeat, this is not itself a textbook – if anything, it is an antidote to textbooks – and one difference is that I will not attempt anything like a comprehensive coverage of 'the literature'. Instead, I will mention those sources which I have found particularly inspiring (or, occasionally, particularly loathsome) to say what I want to say.

Another reason for doing some self-positioning in this introduction is to send a certain sort of signal, which the writing style hopefully reinforces. It is commonplace for books, especially but by no means exclusively textbooks, to be written as if their author were absent or, anyway, detached. The first person is avoided or muted, the book is entitled a 'survey', 'overview' or 'introduction'. This betrays a particular way of thinking about knowledge, not unrelated to the issue of positivism. It is as if the author is irrelevant, a reporter on the field of knowledge, not a participant within it. This makes a kind of sense if organization theory is thought of as science, I suppose. But I think of myself not as a reporter or a scientist but as a commentator or conversationalist. So, as I said a moment ago, this book is meant to initiate a conversation, albeit of a peculiarly narcissistic sort in which I am the only one who gets to speak.

where I am coming from

Having so presumptuously put myself at centre stage, I suppose that I should – and anyway that I can – say a little bit more about myself and in particular about some of the things which have informed the thinking expressed in this book. When I first went to university (Manchester, in 1984) it was to study economics. I liked economics because, I suppose, I had been good at it at school and because it seemed to offer a neat and comprehensible explanation of human behaviour. In classes I sometimes asked my lecturers about the way that economic theories always made assumptions, some of which seemed to be dubious, especially those about rationality. Economics seemed to assume that people somehow formed individual preferences (there was no suggestion that these might be learned or that they might reflect the society in which those individuals had grown up) and that they could and did calculate how to maximize the satisfaction of those preferences. I knew from my own experience that people were often not that rational, myself included. I was told that, in due course, these assumptions would be refined. They never were. Instead, economics as I studied it, and I was fortunate to be taught by excellent teachers who represented the best people in the field, developed a more and more sophisticated mathematics to (allegedly) map and predict human behaviour.

Economics is profoundly influential in the study of organizations and management. Many of the core subjects take on board the assumptions of economics – not just, but certainly including, organization theory. Finance, marketing, operations research and economics itself form the bedrock of management degrees. One of the world's most distinguished organizations theorists, Jim March, who over six decades has provided some of the most influential and sophisticated thinking in the subject, wittily remarked that just as economics suffers from 'physics envy' so too does organization and management theory suffer from 'economics envy' (March, 2000).[4] But the consequence of this is that organization theory, like economics for that matter, says less and less about the people who I know and who, as a matter of fact, actually inhabit organizations.

Having gone to university to study economics, I was obliged to take some other courses in various social science subjects. Initially, these seemed to me to be a waste of time. Not only did I want to study economics, with a view to being an investment banker (or, rather, merchant banker as it was called in those far-off days), but also I was irritated by the way that so many of these other subjects seem to be concerned with vague airy-fairy debates with no definite answer and, apparently, no real *point*. But I came to change my view quite radically.

At more or less the same time I studied, in economics, Coase's theorem with respect to pollution and, in political theory, ideas about power. I make no pretence to representing either of these sets of ideas accurately, not because I am too lazy to look them up but because I want to capture how they struck me at the time.[5] Coase's theorem, as I understood it, said that if a locality was being polluted then those affected, if they didn't like it, would get together and pay the polluter to stop polluting them. Now in one way this chimed with all that I had learnt about economics; in brief and in general, that the way things were was an outcome of the relative values put upon those things by those involved. But, at the same time, I realized that this account of pollution was, in real terms, nonsense. What if those affected did not communicate with each other? What if, having done so, they could not afford to buy off the polluter?

Meanwhile, in my political theory class I was studying power and, by coincidence (or, who knows, by some clever design of the politics lecturers) there was mention of a study of pollution (Crenson, 1971). This study (discussed in Lukes, 1974, a book I still think of as one of the best things ever written in social science) compared two towns in the USA, very similar in all respects except that one had enacted legislation to control a company polluting it whilst the other hadn't. And the explanation of this difference was basically in terms of the local political set-up and power relations between the two towns.

For me, this was something like an epiphany. Economics had offered an explanation that was meant to apply to all people at all times who were faced with pollution. The answer was self-evidently wrong, and in a particular, and very worrying, way. For it implied that if pollution existed then it was because those affected didn't put enough value on the problem to pay to rectify it. This was a fundamentally conservative explanation, of course. Because it said that if there was pollution then it was because no one cared enough to stop it and that if there wasn't it was because enough people were against it to put an end to it. I guess that it was around the same time that I read Voltaire's *Candide* (2001/1759) where the character Pangloss enunciated the philosophy (in real life associated with Leibniz) that the way things are is by definition the best possible outcome ('all is for the best in the best of all possible worlds'), a view stingingly satirized by Voltaire. Thus the hapless Candide, subjected to all kinds of sufferings and humiliations, is given 'panglossian' explanations as to why things must be that way, couldn't be otherwise and that, actually, it was a good thing that they were.

By now sceptical of economics, the political explanation made much more sense to me. If similar towns came to dissimilar solutions then I could see that the explanation could not possibly lie in some general calculus of preferences but in how power was mobilized in different contexts with different results. For example, did people see the pollution as a problem and did they think it could be dealt with? More importantly, did the pollution problem ever get on to the agenda of the local authority or not? What influence did the polluting companies have in each case? I could see that these were real issues, whereas the economic explanation seemed to have no reality at all.

I think that at that point I saw things in terms of better or worse explanations of reality, which is not a bad way to look at things. But subsequently I also came to question whether reality was a good enough test. As I have said, I was a student at Manchester in the 1980s and the biggest political issue then was the miners' strike. Ostensibly the rationale for this was a struggle between the economic reality of the unprofitability of pits and the unrealistic demands of the miners for continued employment. I supported the miners on principle and was involved in a very minor way in various activities including the (probably now forgotten) 'Battle of Brittan' when the then Home Secretary Leon Brittan's visit to Manchester was disrupted by student protestors (of whom I was one) and which led to a violent confrontation with the police, which I well remember (somewhat ingloriously, I ran away and hid in a back garden). But at that point I nevertheless believed that it was true that the pits were uneconomic and my objections to their closure didn't include any denial of this, just a concern about its effects and, from what I can recall, a generalized hostility to all things Thatcherite.[6]

But at the same time that I was hiding in gardens, one of my future PhD supervisors, David Cooper was researching in (what was then) the National Coal Board, looking at accounting practices (Berry et al., 1987). He and his co-workers concluded that the claim that certain pits were uneconomic was founded upon particular ways of making the accounting calculation. Make different assumptions and the reality of the economics of the coal industry was different. And the assumptions made were not grounded in 'reality' but in the interests of various different people involved in the industry. Moreover, the release of these research findings was met with a highly political campaign, albeit unsuccessful, to censor and discredit the researchers. I didn't know about any of this until 1987, when I began PhD work, but when I did it made me realize that knowledge itself was political. It wasn't just, as the Crenson study had shown me, that economic calculations ignored political factors, but that economic calculations were *themselves* political in nature.

I am giving all of this autobiographical detail partly because it helps to explain some of the views expressed in this book. I think that in many ways what I want to urge is a 'political' rather than an 'economic' understanding of organizations. But I have also told this story because I want to explain that the issues I have raised in this book don't come from a kind of 'holier than thou' attitude in which I take some moral high ground. I am – just about – young enough to remember being a student and to remember the worthy, patronizing tedium that I was sometimes subjected to. It's difficult to write a book like this, after years of being an academic, without falling into some of that tone and I know that I have done so. But I do want to try to say that I was once a 19-year-old student, studying economics, not management, but with a pretty similar attitude and set of aspirations to today's average management student (if there is such a thing). I wanted clear, certain knowledge that I could learn to pass exams and give myself a good career. I didn't give up those aspirations for 'politically correct' reasons, but just because they no longer made sense. I changed my view (and my course).

That was almost thirty years ago, but I am still preoccupied with how people do things (organizations, politics, whatever) together, and the gap between the realities of this and the way that conventional academic texts describe it. I think that (some) academic ideas help us to understand everyday life and I don't think that there is a world of theory (books, ideas, models) that is dissociated from practice (getting on with things). For – and how boring this will seem – theory is not the realm of abstract ideas and practice is not the realm of cut-the-crap action.

▨▨▨▨ theory and practice

Let me finish these introductory remarks by saying a bit more about that last point. I have come to think that, in social science, theory is best understood as a way in which people try to pursue particular agendas. Theory is a weapon used to bludgeon others into accepting practice. It almost never reveals that, but still it is true. A good example is the way that Darwinian theory (or, more often, some debased version of Darwinism) is used to justify this or that state of affairs. An example might include the idea that men have evolved to be aggressive and women to be nurturing (I have five sisters, and I can tell you that this is by no means true). Or (closely related) economic theory tells us that the most efficient companies survive because they give better value (never mind that the survival of companies often owes a great deal to their near-monopoly positions – think of Microsoft; or that we often get pretty poor service from companies but the alternatives are all much the same – think of banks). So theory in this way isn't separate from practice; it is a way of, at best, explaining and, at worst, justifying practice. It is 'panglossian' in that it defends the status quo as being unavoidable or, even, more desirable than anything else.

Now of course theory often advances a different agenda, one for change. But always it is about a change in practice. Fundamentally, theory is about mobilizing ideas, arguments and explanations to try to make sense of practice, but also to influence practice. *See* things differently and you will *do* things differently. No sensible person can say 'well, these are just words'. For we all know that words have the power to influence, to move, to inspire, to hurt and to repel people. Think of how you try to win arguments. Words, as one anonymous saying has it, are loaded pistols: we use them at our peril. Ask any politician or for that matter any manager and s/he will tell you that the practice of talking is the most important of their arts and the thing they spend most time doing.

And what about practice? Well, this too is invoked rhetorically. The person who says 'well that is all theory but this is practice' is trying to convince you that the practice is better, more worthwhile, more real than theory could ever be (people only say that about theories they don't like, of course). But practice is always based, even if those involved don't know it, on some kind of theory. The abusive husband slamming his fist into his wife's face (the theory, perhaps, women should know their place); the racist beating up an immigrant (the theory, perhaps, whites are superior); or in organizations, the manager making an employee stay until stopping time (the theory, perhaps, people are lazy and need to know who's boss); or another manager letting a worker go home early (the theory, perhaps, be flexible and people will work harder).

Much organization theory is very closely allied to management practice. It too pursues a particular agenda. It is an agenda which incorporates and validates all kinds of assumptions about organizations, of course, but also about people, politics and ethics – about, in short, how the world we live in is organized. I think, and I will explain why in the book, that it does so in a way which is flawed, highly partial, largely indefensible, and both morally and practically wrong. I mean, if it did work then it would be wrong, but it doesn't work very well anyway.

what you will find in this book

I'm not going to spend too long on this. After all, the whole point of writing a short book is that people can read it, which is obviously the best way of discovering its contents. But I should maybe give some explanation of what it covers and why.

In the first two chapters of the book I talk about what can be called 'classical' issues in the study of organizations. They are classical partly because they are the earliest contributions to the subject we now call organization theory, but they are also classical because they set out a series of themes, issues and ideas which keep recurring in later work, even if in a different language. Sometimes later authors don't realize this, or don't want to (for who wants to hear that their latest thinking just repeats what lies in a dusty corner of the library?). These issues – bureaucratic theory, scientific management and human relations theory – form the bedrock of the knowledge taught on just about every university course on organizations and management. This means that most readers will already have a certain amount of knowledge of them which is helpful to me in my attempt to offer a rather different take on them. And if I can do that successfully then it follows that the same angle can be applied to their recurrence in later work.

In the next three chapters of the book I focus on more contemporary issues in studying organizations. As I've already implied, these grow out of, draw upon and sometimes react against the classical work. They also inform much of the experience of work in organizations during the last thirty years or so. For from the 1980s onwards there has been an apparent acceleration of the influence of organization theory in providing at least a vocabulary of, for example, quality, excellence, empowerment, customer service, flexibility and change which impacts very directly upon organizational life. Anyone who has had a job in recent years will recognize that lexicon. Even those students who have never worked will have seen its effects, say in the way that they now complete evaluations of their lecturers at the end of courses: it's an incarnation of the idea that education is a form of service delivery to customers, something unknown when, say, I was a student. By the way, notice what is going on this example because it is also an example of what I just said about theory and practice. When you fill in the evaluation form it's 'just' a practice, something you do without thinking about it; but it is inseparable from a theory about how to organize education, and a theory which has changed over time (and might change again). Such a development, whilst minor in itself, arises out of the contemporary issues which I discuss in Chapters 3, 4 and 5. I certainly won't cover all the ins and outs of these issues, but want to deal with their common, central features. Thus I will focus in Chapter 3 on organizational culture, which has not just been a theme of contemporary organizational life in its own right but which is also at the heart of a whole range of other initiatives which position 'values' and their management at the heart of organizations. I will then, in Chapter 4, talk about post-bureaucracy as a catch-all term for the range of (supposedly) new organizational forms that (apparently) have supplanted the classical ways of organizing by stressing agility, fluidity and change. Again, students will be familiar with these ideas from their courses but, again, I want to offer a somewhat different angle to that normally taught. In the fifth chapter I try to locate recent developments in organizations within a broader sense of the 'new capitalism' and in particular reflect upon what the financial and economic crisis means for organizations and the study of organizations, and vice versa. It is inevitable that since this crisis is ongoing my analysis can only reflect how things seemed at the time of writing (March 2012). Despite that limitation it is important to me to include this material because part of what I am suggesting here especially, but throughout the book I hope, is that studying organizations is ultimately inseparable from wider political and social issues.

Although each chapter is primarily concerned with a set of ideas about organizations, I have also linked these to an idea about management. As I have already indicated, management is not just part and parcel of organizations but also, in terms of the study of organizations, is often the context and motivation for that study. Organization theory is most often studied inside a management course, and usually by people who are, or who aspire to be, managers. So although there is no automatic or necessary conjunction between organizations and management, I would be foolish if I failed to talk about the contingent connections between the two. In brief, I associate ideas about bureaucracy with scientific management; human relations with people management; culture with self-management; post-bureaucracy with change management; and the new capitalism with some of the strange effects, both positive and negative, of that upon different kinds of management.

These aren't by any means hermetically sealed notions of management, for there are continuities as well as discontinuities between them. Still, they serve to capture how ways of studying organizations link to ways of conceptualizing management.

Finally, conventionally enough, there is a conclusion. But this does more than try to tie things together. Earlier on I mentioned my own passionate conviction about the importance of studying organizations, and I have also tried to show something of the way that that passion was formed. In the conclusion I want to urge again the idea that all of this stuff *matters*, which is why it is, or should be, interesting. It is fundamentally about the kind of world we want to live in. We have choices about that, which ultimately means that studying organizations is not just about what I say to you, and that the conversation is not so one-sided after all. All I can do is to bring what I think is true about studying organizations to your attention. In the end, it is your responsibility what you, as students and as citizens, choose to think is true and how you choose to act upon it.

▬▬▬ notes

1 I have tried to keep end notes to a minimum in this book. But I will just say that all these terms have a currency, contested by scholars. I will use the term 'organization theory' throughout, just to mean the study of organizations. But I don't mean theory rather than practice. Theory/practice is a false distinction. Theory is a practice – doing theory. Practice always involves a theory – some understanding of what is being done and why. But I'll come back to this.

2 By 'critical' I mean the growing approach, usually called Critical Management Studies, which explores the kind of alternative understanding of organizations which informs this book, and which should become clearer in the following pages. See Alvesson and Willmott (1992) for an exposition; Fournier and Grey (2000) for a commentary; and Grey and Willmott (2005) and Alvesson (2011) for collections of key readings.

3 Compare Vroom's (1964) proposition that motivation $M = f$ (E.V) with the statement 'John would have worked hard for promotion, but as there was no chance of promotion he didn't bother'. Face it, the latter is better.

4 This tells us something about the field, but also about the people who work in that field. In this book I make it very clear that I am part and parcel of what I have written. In general, though, writers

on organizations conceal the way that their own identities contribute to the supposedly objective knowledge they produce.

5 So I apologize if I am doing a disservice either to Ronald Coase or to my lecturers.

6 Don't ask me to explain how I reconciled this with my desire to be a merchant banker. I don't know whether I knew at the time, and I certainly can't make sense of it now.

1

Bureaucracy and Scientific Management

It's pretty hard to be efficient without being obnoxious.

Frank McKinney Hubbard

The basis of what I will say in this book is the reading, writing, think-ing, talking and listening about organizations that I have done, origi-nally as an undergraduate student of politics and subsequently as a PhD student and academic in the area of organization theory. I keep coming back to the iconic figure in early organization theory, the German soci-ologist Max Weber (1864–1920). I mention his dates because Weber seems to me very much a man of a particular time. A man of whom it has been said (as it has of others) that he was the last person to know everything of importance that was to be known. A nonsensical idea, of course, but one which points to the extraordinary breadth of his inter-ests in sociology, religion, economics, politics, history, music and much else besides. Nowadays, in common with other academics, organiza-tional theorists restrict themselves to a much narrower canvas and this I think gives organization theory a peculiarly detached feeling. For myself, I don't know where the boundary might be between organization, public administration and political philosophy; or between organization, society, family and individual psychology.

And so I like Max Weber for his breadth and also even for his name, which seems agreeably weighty, Mittel European, *fin de siècle*, whilst also having the kind of panache that might make it a suitable name for a twenty-first century architect or fashion designer. I picture Weber as heavy, bearded, slightly pompous – given to monologues and pro-nouncements of the sort that might begin: 'to understand this question we must in fact analyse it under five headings … '. I have no idea if this is an accurate picture of Weber (although it's true to say that he did have a beard).

Weber saw that what might hold a society together was some sense of authority – that people somehow submitted to the will of others because they believed those others had the right to give the orders. For sure we could envisage a society just held together by brute force, and maybe much of social organization has this as its origin and, permanently, its background. That brute force – call it coercion, call it power – isn't quite the same as authority, though, which connotes people going along with the will of others through consent given on some basis other than just fear. It's a distinction (probed and criticized by many authors) which runs through thinking about organizations.

Some societies or organizations get held together by the charisma of their leaders: the reason why their will is obeyed is because of their characteristic ability to inspire the devotion and obedience of others. There must be a complex psychology here – bred as much by the followers' desires as the leader's charisma – and most candidates for charismatic authority seem peculiar in both good and bad ways. Jesus of Nazareth and Adolf Hitler are usually given as the two poles. Less dramatically, it's commonplace when talking about business leadership nowadays to suggest that it can or should be based on charisma (see Jackson and Parry, 2011). Then again, authority might come from tradition: you obey because that's just the way things are and have always been. The authority of the medieval Church and Royal houses seem like good examples. We can't fully separate out power, charisma and tradition. Inspiring leaders often owe part of their charisma to a propensity to violence; the descendants of such leaders may become imbued with an authority which is purely traditional and, anyway, still backed up with force.

According to Weber, these forms of authority were being increasingly supplanted by something different: rational-legal authority. Here, obedience was secured through a kind of due process: formal, logical, reasoned.[1] Perhaps the key point is that it is not arbitrary – the whims of leaders – but comes from a system. Laws are decided, codified and applied to all citizens. Within organizations, this authority takes the form of rules, procedures and duties. Thus the authority vested in, say, a chief executive is of a particular sort. First it comes from the job itself, not the person. We obey (if we do) the chief executive because s/he holds that job and not (or not primarily) because of the person's charisma or membership of a particular family. When a new person takes on that role, the authority transfers to them. And the role places a limit on what kinds of obedience can be called for. Again, it is not arbitrary. As an academic I can legitimately ask a student to write an essay but not to clean my shoes.

The kind of organization which emerges from the complete application of the rational-legal principle is one which is entirely defined by rules and a series of hierarchical relationships – a bureaucracy. People's jobs were defined: you did the book-keeping but didn't clean the toilets. Then they were refined: you cleaned the toilets on the first floor, someone else did the second floor. And the more the organization grew, the more refined were the jobs. Then again, you didn't do the jobs any old how. What was important was to do them in a way established for you by rules. That way, it was possible to be certain that the job was being done in the most efficient manner. In this sense, rational-legal organization entails the removal of discretion – i.e. judgement or choice – from work. You worked under orders from those above you in the hierarchy and reported to them. The removal of discretion and the fact that authority comes from the role and not the person means that another kind of arbitrariness disappears as well: appointment to a job and promotion were based strictly on experience and qualifications.

Although in many ways not a bureaucracy, something of this process can be seen when, for example, a group of students share a house. Often they will draw up a rota defining who will do chores like cleaning and cooking (all too often a document which experience shows to have been hopelessly optimistic). It defines responsibilities and it is usually animated by some notion of fairness, such that the work is shared equally. It may also be attentive to the particular skills that individuals have (for example, ability to cook). As I say, this isn't a bureaucracy but it shows how even a very simple organization can make use of principles of systemization, division of labour and authority. We would think it odd and, a key point, *illegitimate* if household chores were allocated on the basis of physical coercion by the strongest person.

Weber was by no means a partisan for the emergence of rational-legal or bureaucratic organizations. On the contrary, he seems to have been alarmed by their rapid spread through the state, business and institutions to the point where he feared that the world was becoming enclosed in an 'iron cage' of rationalization. But why were they becoming dominant? Because, says Weber, they represent the most technically efficient and rational form of organization.

what is rationality?

This proposition, its meaning and difficulties seem to me to be defining of a whole set of issues which have resonated through both organization theory and practice ever since. It might almost be said that there is a fault line on organization theory which doesn't just stem from, but runs through, Max Weber. The crucial issue is what it means to be rational. That is a big question and I am not a philosopher (and, in any case, philosophers do not agree on the answer). Roughly speaking, one of the key shifts in human history was that period, around the last half of the eighteenth century, when Enlightenment philosophy emerged, along with empirical science and industrial production. That philosophy was committed to secular rather than religious explanation and the idea that the application of reason rather than tradition or dogma would not only better explain the world but also allow its improvement. In one way, this was extraordinarily emancipating. The philosopher Immanuel Kant, in his 1784 essay 'What is Enlightenment?' (in Reiss, 1991), says that enlightenment lies in daring to know, in having the courage to use one's own reason rather than rely upon the authority of others. This could be said to be *the* foundational text of modern Western thought.

Yet the rationality envisaged by bureaucracy seems to be the exact opposite of this, for it is precisely the use of one's own reason which is prohibited when the capacity for discretion is removed. Take away arbitrary conduct (which presumably includes both rational and irrational conduct) and you also take away the capacity for the individual use of reason. The rationality of bureaucracy resides in the system of rules, not in the judgement of individuals, except those, usually high up in the organization, who make the rules and who do retain discretion to some degree. And so from its inception, bureaucracy sets up a dichotomy of systemic and individual rationality.

Max Weber identified another kind of dichotomy. Bureaucracies are rational in one particular sense of the word – formal or instrumental rationality. The idea here is that the means adopted to achieve a particular end are the most efficient for that purpose. This might mean that they minimize wastage and maximize production. And so, although bureaucracy nowadays connotes inefficiency and red tape, its Weberian form suggests otherwise. Yes, there are rules, but these are the price to pay for avoiding the calamities that come from not following the rules. Interestingly, current-day attempts to reduce bureaucracy so as to foster innovation frequently run into appalling disasters when, freed from rule-following, organizations take risks which do not come off – the 'light touch' regulation of financial markets and the subsequent crisis, discussed in Chapter 5, being one example. Flexibility, too, has its price tag. For Weber, the bureaucracy with its machine-like operation, its complete harmony of individual actions untainted by discretion, could routinely outperform any other kind of organization. Small wonder that it was taking over the world.

Weber's other kind of rationality was substantive or value rationality. Here the question was whether the 'ends' of action were in and of themselves rational. Thus, suppose that I decide to murder someone at random. This is substantively irrational – the end or purpose is irrational, the act of a madman. But if I do so with a swift karate blow to the heart, this is formally rational (it is the most efficient means) despite being substantively irrational. However, if I proceed by slapping my victim with a wet fish for several days, then this is neither formally nor substantively rational. Bureaucracies are formally rational but they don't do substantively rational. That does not mean that they are *never* substantively rational, but it does means that they may not be. They simply don't consider that domain of rationality because they are not concerned with ends, only with means.

My murder example sounds like a silly one, but it has a horrifying real-world counterpart in the Nazi Holocaust. According to Zygmunt Bauman's extraordinary book *Modernity and the Holocaust* (1989), the genocide instigated by the Nazis represents the extreme application of a bureaucratic logic. For what makes the Holocaust so peculiarly appalling is the way in which it was conducted industrially – with a system of rules, impersonally applied, which made it as technically efficient as genocide could be. The capacity to register and monitor populations – Jews, Communists, gypsies, homosexuals and the other 'categories' to which the Nazis were so murderously opposed – was itself a considerable administrative achievement. The shipping of these people to the camps was another, and their systematic extermination a third. One of my favourite authors, the novelist C.P. Snow, has one of his characters, a wartime civil servant in London, reflect that, just as he was handling the memoranda relating to the development of atomic weapons, so his counterpart in Berlin would be reviewing figures on the death rate of Jewish people under different dietary regimes (this was written before the extermination programme was known about, although the existence of concentration camps was). Bureaucratic practice, the impersonal, scientific, ethically neutral pursuit of means made the Holocaust *formally* rational whilst, clearly, not being substantively rational. Bauman says that we should not, therefore, see the Holocaust as an aberration or anomaly when compared with mainstream Western culture: rather, it was a manifestation of the habitual ways of organizing within that culture. For sure this is an extreme case, but its logic is very common and is found whenever we detach ends from means – and if it is a case that seems extreme and remote now, remember that it was very real indeed as recently as our parents' and grandparents' generation.

Once we move from the extreme cases, life gets more difficult. For who is to say what is substantively rational? It is a question of values and, whereas there are some values which are so widely shared as to approach universality (so that we can agree about the Holocaust), there are far more cases where there is little or no agreement. This was perhaps not as difficult for Weber as it is for us today. Weber, who had inherited the Enlightenment tradition of Kant, would have hoped that ethics could itself be made the subject of rational judgement. Whereas religions addressed ethics through the authority of tradition, backed up by the not inconsiderable weight of the will of God, post-Enlightenment societies have had to make do with a secularly derived ethics. For Kant, this would be to say that it would be irrational to act in a way which you would not wish to be the way that people generally acted. In other words – do as you would be done by. This still has its appeal, but it (and other attempts at a rational basis for ethics) has real limitations. In particular, people may have quite different views about how they themselves would like to be treated.[2] One of the defining features of contemporary society seems to be a fragmentation of ethics. So substantive rationality turns out to mean a social consensus about values and that consensus does not, to any great extent, exist. We may overwhelmingly agree that genocide is wrong; we don't agree about abortion or euthanasia.

Anyway, all this aside, the fundamental point is that bureaucracies don't care about substantive rationality, they don't care about ethics, they are just about getting the job done as quickly as possible. That doesn't mean that they couldn't, in fact, be doing an ethically good job (for example, a charity). They could; just as easily as they could be doing an ethically poor one. It's just that this would be irrelevant, either way, to bureaucratic logic. But is this true? One of the most interesting books on organizations, Paul du Gay's *In Praise of Bureaucracy* (2000), argues otherwise. Amongst many other points, he says that formally rational bureaucracies do embody a specific and very important ethic. In rejecting patronage and promoting impersonality, bureaucracies are about *fairness*. Being employed or promoted does not depend upon whether you went to the same school as the boss, or the colour of your skin, or whether you agree to sleep with your manager. The service you receive as a client or customer is not conditioned by the mood or prejudice of the person giving the service, or any other value judgements.

I think du Gay is right in what he says. My only caveat would be that he is only right in relation to what Weber called ideal-type bureaucracies, or at least close fits. An ideal-type is the fullest, purest, most complete version of an idea, concept or practice. It doesn't mean that Weber thought that bureaucracies were an ideal to be strived for – as I mentioned earlier he worried about them. But in the pure bureaucracy, there is, as Paul du Gay says, an ethic of fairness, transparency, accountability and 'due process'. The problem is that actual bureaucracies do not necessarily – and, moreover, often do not – embody this ethic.

bureaucratic dysfunctionalism

To understand this, I find it helpful to think about a set of classic studies of bureaucracy, sometimes called the 'bureaucratic dysfunctionalist' literature. One of my many objections to organization theory at the present time is its perverse belief that anything published before, say, 2000 – if that – is boring, old hat and that it is somehow shameful to consider it. The fact that many of today's 'contributions to the literature' do no more than anaemically repeat earlier work is, of course, merely a reflection of my old age (I was 46 when I wrote these words). The fact that I have a suspicion that many of the earlier studies were based upon more serious programmes of empirical investigation and thought is similarly antediluvian. But enough of that hobby horse.

The bureaucratic dysfunctionalists suggest that bureaucracies in practice have not just the problem of a deficit of substantive rationality but, even, a deficit of formal rationality. Crozier's (1964) study of French bureaucracy shows how, contrary to du Gay, bureaucrats continue to indulge their own prejudices and preferences in their conduct. They were no more ideal-typical than Melville Dalton's *Men who Manage* (1959) who managed to find considerations of gender, race, religion and suburb relevant to their decision-making. Two decades later, Rosabeth Moss Kanter, before she became a management guru, found that managers in a bureaucracy liked to appoint those who shared their own background, gender and education (Kanter, 1977), and this 'homosociality' of recruitment continues to occur in many contemporary organizations despite attempts at equal opportunity and diversity initiatives.

To continue, Gouldner's (1954) investigation of a gypsum mine revealed the presence of 'mock bureaucracy', where an impressive array of rules and regulations, the hallmark of formal rationality, existed. The only problem was that they were ignored. It's common (and this was one of Gouldner's examples) to have safety regulations that staff don't, in fact, respect. A friend and colleague of mine once researched equal opportunities for women in organizations. 'All taken care of ', he was told. 'We have a policy' – and a large manual of equal opportunities procedures was proudly displayed. But, my colleague asked, were there in fact equal opportunities for women? Procedures and practices aren't necessarily the same thing.

This idea, that there might be a disjuncture between the formal rules of a bureaucracy and what actually happens, is given an elegant twist in the work of Blau (1955). He noted that one of the most potent weapons in the arsenal of trade unions is the 'work to rule'. Here, workers agree only to follow the letter of what they are obliged to do by contract and job description. Why? To disrupt the organization in pursuit of a union aim, perhaps a pay rise. Yet if following the rules is *disruptive*, it cannot be the case that these rules do indeed prescribe the most efficient of outcomes. Instead, there is a gap between the rules and what people actually do that contributes to efficiency and, therefore, formal rules and efficiency are not identical.

Perhaps the 'daddy' of bureaucratic dysfunctionalism is Merton's (1940) argument about 'goal displacement'. Bureaucracies have an inbuilt tendency, because they focus on means and not ends, to degenerate into a situation where the means becomes an end in itself. In other words, following the rule becomes the point, not the point of the rule. Suppose a security guard is taking care of a factory. He (let us assume it is a man) is told to follow a rule, and the rule is that no one is to be admitted without a pass. The purpose or end of the rule is to protect the factory. The means is the security guard checking passes. One fine day the Managing Director arrives early for a meeting. The factory is in trouble and the MD is meeting with creditors. But she (let us assume it is a woman) has not brought her pass. The security guard recognizes the MD, of course, but will not let her enter without a pass. Rules, he says, are rules. So the MD fails to make the meeting and the factory closes down. The security guard's goal or end (protecting the factory) has been displaced, so that the means (checking passes) has become an end in itself. Thus formal rationality swallows up substantive rationality, and systemic rationality overwhelms individual rationality.

formal and informal; intended and unintended

All of these examples and arguments serve to point up two interesting things. Both of them seem to me to be central to understanding anything much about organizations. The first is that there is a disjuncture between the formal and the informal organization. Trivial examples might be that 'formally' you have to be at work by 9 am, or that you cannot use work Internet access for private purposes, but 'informally' you don't have to be in exactly on time, or can use the Internet privately if you're not busy and don't do it too much. The formal organization of rules, procedures, what is 'meant to' happen, is not the same as the organization itself. The organization itself includes – and in some senses it *is* – what actually happens. This could mean that bureaucracy is less efficient than Weber anticipated and less ethical than du Gay hopes. It means that alongside impersonal rules and procedures we have to consider highly personal prejudices, motivations and actions.

It means something else, too. Bureaucracy has been criticized for dehumanizing people. It is not hard to see why. In the ideal-type, people are no more than parts in a well-oiled machine – devoid of discretion, passion, prejudice and personality. Devoid, in a sense, of agency – the capacity to make choices and act. Yet, for good or ill, this is not so once we recognize the informal aspect of organization. Instead, the recalcitrant or complaining, lazy or hardworking, laughing or frowning, pretty or ugly, trusting or cynical *person* comes back into focus. I will say much more about this later, but for now I will just make one caveat. The formal and informal organization are not unrelated, independent spheres; they are interdependent and mutually constitutive; one could not exist without the other, and the precise nature in any particular case of the one will influence the other.

Then there is a second implication, especially arising from goal displacement. What is done in organizations – for example, establishing rules – will always carry with it the possibility, and, in fact, near certainty, of having both intended and unintended consequences. This idea is a very powerful one. It suggests that whenever people act towards some purpose, the outcomes will be a mixture of what was hoped for by the action and what was unforeseen and possibly undesired. Think of a situation where there are disruptions to petrol supplies. An individual with, perhaps, a half tank of petrol may think it sensible to fill up. But many other individuals make the same (rational) decision. Result? Huge queues at petrol stations, which run out, which causes more disruption to supply and more panic buying and so on. This is an unintended consequence of individual action.

Unintended consequences are perhaps most important when we think about management (and, as I said in the Introduction, that currently is the context in which organizations are most often studied). They mean that the capacity of managers to get things done is often confounded and, moreover, that much of management consists of dealing with the unintended consequences of previous actions. But, since that 'dealing with' will itself give rise to further unintended consequences, this means that management – and organization generally – is perennially failing in the sense that its ends are never finally achieved. Such a prospect means that, other issues aside, the idea of a bureaucratic organization – or any other kind of organization – being simply about the establishment of appropriate means to reach given ends is fundamentally, irredeemably and irrevocably flawed.

These claims run so counter both to the social image of the manager and to what is taught in most management schools that I should elaborate a little more on unintended consequences. Why do they arise? At least one part of this has already been prefigured. The fact that people have some degree of agency means that it is open to them to ignore, resist, circumvent or just plain misunderstand; all of which will make the best-laid management plans go awry. There has long been a debate in the social sciences about the nature and extent of agency.[3] The so-called structure–agency or structure–action dualism has as its two poles the propositions that social structures effectively determine what happens, and people have little, or no, individual effect or – on the agency side – that all we have is individuals making choices, and social structure is just the aggregate of these. So, for example, debate about crime often polarizes between those who say that crime levels are effectively determined by the extent of poverty, unemployment and social deprivation (structure) and those who see it entirely in terms of individual decisions as to whether or not to commit a crime (agency).

Whilst, both in some social science and much everyday life, analysis is polarized between structure and agency, much social theory in the last few decades has, in various different ways, suggested that it is a false dichotomy. Structure–agency is not an either/or but a both/and. Anthony Giddens (1984), for example, has proposed a duality of structure and action so that action reproduces structure whilst structure conditions and shapes action. The classic example is language. To speak a language in a way that others understand means following the existing rules, or structure, of language that existed before we were born and which we must learn and adhere to. Yet, at the same time, a language only exists because individuals speak it and, as a matter of fact, they constantly adopt new words, slang and ways of speaking, which is why language changes over time. In this sense, language users are agents or actors but they both exist within, and enact, the structures of the language they speak.

Thus, in an organization, what people do is certainly conditioned by the rules, procedures and norms prevailing, but these only continue to exist, and develop, because of the actions, choices and behaviours of individuals. Students sit in a lecture hall, following the social rules or structure that determine that they should be there and behave in a certain way and their lecturer similarly follows rules. But in choosing to do this, students and lecturer alike 'reproduce' the social rules or structure through their choice or agency. This seems to me a sensible approach, and it means that agency can never be written out of organizations and so the perfect machine-like organization is a myth. We cannot necessarily predict what people will do.

And there is more to the issue of prediction than simply the question of people's individuality. The added complexity is that people will behave differently precisely because of the predictions which are made about them. This is one of the principle reasons why there is a disjuncture between social and natural sciences (a disjuncture denied by positivists). If I make a prediction about the behaviour of a natural object, it may or may not come true, depending upon how well-founded my scientific theories are; but the outcome will not be affected by the fact of my having made a prediction.[4] But consider something like the housing market. I am thinking of selling my house but want to wait until prices have reached their highest. I read in the paper that prices are set to peak and so put my house on the market. But so do many other people. The result is that there is an increase in supply and prices begin to fall. The prediction has been self-fulfilling. Or suppose I read that prices have peaked and are now falling. I hold off selling my house and so do others. The result is a decrease of supply and prices begin to rise. The prediction has been confounded.[5] There is, in the social world, no way of separating out our theories and predictions about the world from what happens in the world. This is one of the reasons why the predictions of economists, upon which government budgeting is based, so often turn out wrong.

What applies to the social world in general is also true in organizations. Suppose I hear that a new chief executive is being appointed who has a reputation for sacking people. I might decide to look for a new job and leave before I am fired. I might decide to work very hard in the hope that the axe will fall elsewhere. I might decide to work less hard as I think I am likely to lose my job anyway. Predictions about the future change conduct and therefore affect what actually happens in the future; again, this is not true in predictions made about inanimate objects. In a similar way, assumptions about people can have strange effects. I will talk more about this later, but, for now, consider the case of a manager who assumes that the workforce is motivated solely by money. Accordingly, a pay system is devised with, for example, bonuses for good performance. In these circumstances the assumption is likely to be self-fulfilling in that the workforce, offered only the motivation of money, will be motivated only by money. Their commitment to the quality of work or the company itself will be limited or non-existent.

An important factor implicit in all this is that organizations, like life in general, take place in time. We cannot imagine an equilibrium point. To continue with my previous example, suppose in response to a materialistic workforce a new human resource manager is appointed. She thinks the answer is to give the workforce more freedom and responsibility. Some of them, used to the previous style, respond by taking advantage of this to slack off. In the meantime, others leave and are replaced by people who have only known the new system. But by now the slackers are a problem and the manager tightens up. The new workers are now resentful. But anyhow, by now the company has been taken over and a new management system is being introduced – and so it continues. There is no one point at which a supposedly optimum system of organization can be reached and, again, this means that the solutions to problems at any one time form the basis of new problems in the future. This dynamic, temporal character of organizations is again a reason for plans being confounded and unintended consequences arising. In this sense, rather than thinking about organizations as fixed entities, it might be better to think of them as current manifestations of an ongoing process of *organizing* (see, for example, Weick, 1979).

These kinds of issues – agency, unpredictability, goal displacement and, overall, unintended consequences – are the irreducible core of organization. They are not anomalies and anyone who works in an organization or reads the news will know how pervasive they are. For example, at one point in the British education system, attempts were made to set targets for attainment so that schools should achieve a 25 per cent target for A–C grades in GCSE. The purpose was to ensure that all pupils, not just the highest achievers, are catered for. But consider the school at 23 per cent. There the teacher's best hope of reaching the target is to concentrate effort on the 2 per cent of the class falling just outside the target and to neglect everyone else (see Gewirtz, 2002, for detail). So wider educational attainment (the goal or substantially rational end) got lost or was displaced by the pursuit of a specific target (the formally rational means). Similarly, in the NHS, attempts to shorten waiting lists (with the goal of improving health outcomes and well-being) by introducing target times were confounded by hospitals creating waiting lists for waiting lists and thereby meeting the target. These and endless other examples that could be given are the real world effects of the 'theoretical' ideas of unintended consequences, goal displacement and the subordination of substantive rationality to formal rationality. Yet the irony is that these effects are then usually treated as a new problem, demanding new targets, new measures, new ways of organizing, which then go on to create their own unintended consequences. It is in this sense that organizations and management are perennially failing. And this is not because managers are stupid or ill-intentioned, it is because they fail to give sufficient attention to unintended consequences and so on; a failure which is not so much because of a lack of 'theoretical' knowledge but a lack of realism about practice.

▰▰▰ so what?

I suppose that there is a big 'so what?' to all of this. After all, if this is true, what are we to do? Just give up trying to organize? That seems tricky if organization is in some way endemic to human culture. Perhaps we just have to accept unintended consequences and get on with it if there is no alternative. I don't have any straightforward answers to this but, at the very least, I think that simply to recognize the issues takes us a long way forward. First off, it might call forth a degree of humility from, in particular, managers and politicians. Too often they act as if they can deliver perfect solutions. Relatedly, it suggests the need for a degree of care. Unintended consequences may always be with us, but some are more foreseeable than others. Confronted with a problem, managers often too quickly and too confidently announce that the answer is simple: a reorganization; a new inventory system; a new accounting system; a new reward system. This is a conceit often fed by management consultants, gurus and indeed business schools.

Encountering a call for more deliberation, the response will typically be that there is no time to do so – but this is surely irresponsible, and to some large extent the busy-ness of managers is simply self-perpetuating, since it leads to ill-considered changes which then produce problems which, in turn, keep managers constantly busy. At one time I was involved in preparing some recommendations for research policy to be presented to a government minister (I am deliberately keeping the details vague). 'But remember', his civil servants cautioned, 'the minister is a very busy man, and will want to be presented with a short list of bullet points'. Yet one might have thought that since the policy area involved the expenditure of many millions of pounds, and since even the process of developing the recommendations had cost many thousands of pounds, the minister might have been well-advised to spend a little longer so as to understand the complexities of the matter in hand. Additionally, and related to time, one feature of managerial (and indeed ministerial) careers is that people have often moved jobs before the unintended consequences they have created become manifest. This in itself is a recipe for irresponsibility (one might say it is an unintended consequence of the design of managerial careers).

However, there are much wider implications for what I have tried to say so far in this chapter. Ultimately, we cannot conceive of a form of organization and management in which means are detached from ends (and I mean here both goals and effects, both intended and unintended). For this is to detach organization from ethics and values. In the Introduction to this book I said that my approach to organization theory is in some ways 'anti-management', and the ultimate reason for this is that it seems to me that much or most writing on organizations and management does purport to detach means from ends and does ignore, or significantly truncate, attention to ethics and values. I want now to elaborate that thought a bit more, this time by talking about some of the origins of management thought and practice, origins which have left an enduring legacy to the present day.

Taylorism and scientific management

To do this, I will introduce another of the iconic figures from organization theory, from a similar time to Max Weber, but a man of a very different stamp: Frederick Winslow Taylor. Taylor (1856–1917) was no theorist, he was an engineer working in one of the toughest of industries (iron and steelmaking) during one of the most remarkable periods of technical and managerial innovation the world has seen: the industrialization of the United States following the American Civil War. In one way, it was remarkable that Taylor was doing this job at all. Born into a wealthy Philadelphia family, he seemed destined for a career in the law when he took the unusual decision to go into the steel business, initially as an apprentice. His childhood had been rigidly controlled, with all his activities – sport, walking, sleeping position and country dancing – minutely analysed and prescribed (Fineman, 1996: 545).

This might lead us to understand his life's work in primarily psychological terms, but this would be mistaken to the extent that it was also historically rooted (structure and agency again). For one thing that is worth saying at the outset is that a great many other people, many of them engineers, were developing similar ideas to Taylor at a similar time in a similar place. But it is Taylor's name that has become inseparable from this general movement, usually known as 'scientific management'. By recognizing that this *was* a general movement, it is possible to see that it reflected a particular set of problems, assumptions and attitudes; it did not emerge by chance, and its context is really quite important.

Pennsylvania in and around the 1870s was a revolutionary place.[6] Its smokestacks bore testament to industry on a scale and pace that had never been seen before, even in the English Industrial Revolution. It is almost no exaggeration to say that it was out of this cockpit that management, and a good part of what has defined human society since, at least in the West, emerged. It did so in a form which gave management what Yehouda Shenhav (1999), in one of the finest historical studies of the subject, has called its engineering legacy. It is surely no coincidence that it was also in Pennsylvania that the world's first business school,

Wharton, was founded in 1881, nor that Joseph Wharton was both the founder of that school and the owner of one of Taylor's workplaces.

The steel industry (and others) was in large part the creation of immigrants and in ways which had an interesting pattern, right from the beginning. The mill owners and many of the engineers were often from Scottish families and were often (like Taylor) Protestant or Nonconformist in religion. Weber knew all about Taylor, and regarded his work as emblematic of the advance of rationalized organization. And Weber (1992) had also advanced the thesis that Protestantism, with its values of thrift, hard work and individualism, had a particular affinity with the development of capitalism. The US steel industry bore this out. The workers in the mills, however, typically had a different background. In the early years, they were more likely to be Irish emigrants and to be Catholics. Later, they came from all parts of Europe and spoke a huge variety of languages. It is no small part of the context of scientific management that it emerged as an artefact to the relationship between Protestants and Catholics and English and non-English speakers: it is overlaid by cultural and racial assumptions. It's also worth saying that steel was an overwhelmingly male, and even macho, industry, and this too left its mark on management.

Taylor (I'll cease from now on to remember others doing the same thing) identified a problem based on his early experience as a machine operator. He was working in some of the biggest of the iron and steel plants, at Midvale and Bethlehem (this was the one owned by Joseph Wharton) in Pennsylvania, and his problem was one which is familiar to anyone who, like me, knows nothing about cars. When I go to the garage to have my car fixed, the mechanic may say to me – sucking in air through his[7] teeth – that I have a serious problem, that it will take several days to fix, and that it will cost me a large amount of money. I have no way of knowing if this is true. I don't know what the fault is, I don't know if it could be fixed more quickly, I don't know what parts will be needed. What I do about all this will in large part depend upon the extent to which I trust the mechanic.

Taylor's problem was similar. He was working in an industry where it was normal for workers to organize their own work. Work gangs hired their own crew, worked at their own pace, used their own tools and, crucially, knew far more about the work than did their supervisors. Work was assigned and done on a rule of thumb or 'guesstimate' basis. Taylor reckoned that workers tended to, as he called it, 'soldier'; he meant that they slacked off, either because of 'natural soldiering' – they were naturally lazy and would work as little as they could – or 'systematic soldiering' – they would deliberately restrict output so as to keep their jobs and maximize staff levels for themselves and their friends. It's noticeable that this implies that Taylor didn't trust the workers much, and here the cultural context is important: it reflects in part the stereo-typical attitude of work ethic Puritans towards the supposedly feckless and dishonest Catholics.

The solution lay in scientific management, which Taylor articulated in many different ways but most famously in his four principles, famil-iar no doubt to every student of management and organizations:

- A science of each element of work.
- Scientific selection and training of workers.
- Division of labour between workers and managers.
- Co-operation between managers and workers.

In practice what the first of these meant was time and motion (T&M) studies. T&M meant managers using a stopwatch and standing over a worker to measure the time taken for each tiny component of the job being done. Imagine the act of drinking a glass of beer:

Start position: Standing at bar
Movement 1: Hand to glass (2 seconds)
Movement 2: Grip glass (0.5 seconds)
Movement 3: Lift to horizontal (1 second)
Movement 4: Lift to lips (1 second)
Movement 5: Swallow 0.05 litres beer (2 seconds)
Movement 6: Move arm to horizontal (1 second)
Movement 7: Move glass to bar (1 second)
Movement 8: Release grip on glass (0.5 seconds)
Movement 9: Belch (1 second)
End position: Standing at bar
Total time
for operation: 10 seconds

In practice, of course, it would be an industrial process operation but the principle is the same. It establishes the optimum time for the operation with no wastage (from the point of view of the operation itself) from other activities: no pausing to smile, or pick up a cigarette, or pop to the loo or eye-up the person next to you at the bar. It is easy to see why this technique attracted Weber's attention, for it is an exemplar of formal rationality.

Having established the time for each motion in the process, it becomes possible to set benchmarks. If one operation can be completed in 10 seconds then 6 can be done in a minute, 360 in an hour and 2,880 in an eight-hour shift. And a pay rate for the shift could be set, with a bonus for exceeding it and a pay cut for failing to reach it. Of course, in the beer drinking example, or in an industrial process, you might say that the rate that the operation can be done might decrease over time. But this was no problem for scientific management: it measured, and factored in, fatigue time.

At a stroke, this system solved the soldiering problem by effecting a very fundamental redistribution of power. No longer was it possible for workers to give unrealistic estimates of the time needed to perform a task. How long will it take to drink half a litre of beer? 100 seconds – no more and no less. The manager with the stopwatch now has the power, not the person performing the task.

I have chosen the example of beer drinking as an illustration because we would normally think of something like having a drink as an unregulated activity over which we ourselves have choice, and this, to a degree, was how industrial work was, pre-Taylorism.[8] The impact, or more accurately the intention, of Taylorism and scientific management was to evacuate all discretion from work processes so that the organization would become akin to machines and workers akin to machine parts.

That workers were regarded as no more than components in the organizational machine is important. It reflects very much an engineering mindset, in which the machine was an obvious model and metaphor. It perhaps reflects a derogatory attitude towards the supposedly almost less than human Catholics and foreigners that comprised the workforce. But it also reflects a pragmatism: these techniques overcame many of the problems of communication between people who spoke different languages. Perhaps most interesting of all, it reflected a particular kind of ethic, in a way which recalls du Gay's defence of bureaucracy. For Taylor believed that his system embodied an impersonal fairness: the fairness of 'a fair day's wage for a fair day's work'. It is easy to understand how this might be. Workers would no longer be dependent upon the patronage of a work gang leader, but would be paid and worked according to a fixed system. This would be of particular importance to, for example, an immigrant worker from Eastern Europe faced with the established position of an Irish foreman hiring and firing from within his own ethnic group. It is also the case that Taylor's system could make for a safer workplace. At a time when industrial injuries were rife, a system that devised a standard way of working which, if followed, would not just be more productive but would avoid accidents did have an appeal for workers. Taylorism has its problems, as I will explain, but it would be overly facile to completely dismiss the specifically ethical claims which Taylor made for it.

On the other hand, as one of the most prominent and insightful critics of the Taylorist system, Harry Braverman (1974) points out, for Taylor a fair day's work meant the maximum amount of work a person could physically do without collapsing, and a fair day's pay meant the minimum amount that could be paid to induce the worker to give this level of effort. Braverman remarks that you might just as well say that a fair day's work would be that amount of work which produces an output of equivalent value to what the worker is paid. But if that were so, the process would not yield a profit. Thus, from Braverman's perspective, scientific management must be understood in terms of its value to capitalist profit-seeking and not as any kind of fairness.

The introduction of scientific management provoked an enormous reaction. It is tempting from a current-day perspective to see it as a natural and unremarkable development in industrial organization. Because it, in fact, happened, it's tempting to think it *had* to happen. But that it happened was the outcome of a struggle which at the time did not seem determined, any more than present-day arguments about how to organize have a preordained outcome. Shenhav (1999) shows how scientific management was a part of a whole 'standardization movement' (which included things like the standardization of tool sizes and machine parts) which was bitterly contested. Many critics said that standardization was inimical to American individualism, and would sap innovation and entrepreneurship.

Taylorism, specifically, was extensively resisted by workers and their embryonic trade unions. It is not hard to see why. The system entailed a massive transfer of power from workers to managers. It reduced autonomy, eroded working conditions and threatened unemployment (as more could be done with fewer people). Fundamentally, as Braverman and many others have explained, Taylorism implemented a radical and near complete separation between conception and execution, meaning planning and decision-making, on the one hand, and carrying out orders on the other. This was the division of labour set out in Taylor's principles. Managers would decide, workers would act accordingly. One of the key decisions was over the hiring and training of workers, previously carried out by the work group itself. This is why Taylor's principle included the scientific selection and training of workers. Given all of this, the meaning of Taylor's final principle, co-operation between managers and workers, was a rather truncated one: workers had to undertake to do the work in the prescribed manner in return for the wages on offer (or fines for noncompliance), and leave everything else to the managers.

Everywhere that scientific management was introduced it caused conflict. Workers went on strike or left their jobs, and T&M studies were actually banned in US defence plants. Interestingly, it was not just workers who reacted against Taylorism. Owners and some senior managers objected too. For the system created a new breed of powerful managers, mainly production engineers. If, previously, workers had had the power that came from knowledge of how to do work, now it was these engineers who had privileged access to a baffling array of new knowledge. With their stopwatches, their myriad sheets of benchmarks and pay rates, they presented a threat not just to workers but owners and some managers. Taylor himself was sacked, because his employers did not appreciate the industrial unrest his system engendered. Embittered, he insisted that his ideas had not been properly implemented. But, importantly, he inspired a devoted group of followers who propagated and developed his ideas well into the twentieth century.

If the development of scientific management was contested, the watershed came with the First World War (1914–18). Now there was a patriotic imperative to maximize production of armaments.[9] Workers and others were asked to set aside their reservations in the interests of the war effort and, by and large, they agreed. But once the war was over, these methods were established and maintained. That is not to say that resistance ceased. On the contrary, Taylorist systems continued to provoke a wide array of responses. Sabotage, absenteeism and high staff turnover were the most obvious but more insidious, perhaps, was the tendency of such systems to breed low commitment and low quality.

What was going on here was a kind of unintended consequence of a type I indicated earlier. Taylorism treated workers as being motivated in a very simple way – carrot and stick, or pain and pleasure. There were targets: exceed them and gain a bonus, fail to meet them and get a fine. This idea that people are motivated solely by money had a self-fulfilling quality. If money was all that was on offer, then money could be all that mattered. Why should the workers care if what they produced was shoddy, why should they be committed to the product or to the company if they were simply treated as money-motivated robots? They did not. Instead, they churned out their product, got their bonuses (or didn't) and looked elsewhere for the things that made life worthwhile. In some cases, this was no more than the end-of-week drinking session. In others, it took the form of a remarkable flourishing of working-class culture in industrial areas. In Britain, the choirs of South Wales, the brass bands of Yorkshire colliery towns, the art clubs and mechanics institutes of many nineteenth- and twentieth-century towns are just some examples. The activities of trade unions and, later, the Communist Party were more political consequences. Much later, as these areas became de-industrialized, these activities in turn collapsed, which showed that they were indeed a by-product of industrial organization, leaving a cultural vacuum often either left hollow or filled with a diet of drugs, crime and 'reality' TV. In all of these ways, be it noted, 'work organizations' and 'society' are so deeply intertwined as to be inseparable, and so it is impossible to study the one without the other, a major and recurring theme of this book.

The evacuation of meaning from work also had implications from a managerial perspective. That so little energy and commitment went into work, that the quality of products was no longer a matter of pride to workers constituted the backdrop to much that was to happen in the management of organizations during the twentieth century and beyond (as I said earlier, yesterday's solutions are often the source of today's problems). But that lesson was a long time in coming, and even then was learnt in ways which reflected the engineering legacy of scientific management, as I will discuss in subsequent chapters. In the meantime, what actually happened was an intensification of the Taylorist approach with the introduction of a system which, being pioneered at the Ford motor company, carries the unsurprising name of Fordism.

The Fordist system added a crucial innovation to that of Taylorism: the moving assembly line. Here, a mechanically driven conveyor belt brings the work to the worker, who stands at a fixed work station and performs a small operation upon the car (as it was at Ford) before it moves down to the next operative, until the finished product emerges at the other end. The moving assembly line entails a massive simplification of the Taylor system because a huge number of those bodily movements which hitherto had to be prescribed by the T&M study were now mechanized. Workers were even more than before rendered as parts within the organizational machine. Moreover, it became possible for managers to gain greater control of the rate of work through the simple expedient of speeding up the conveyor belt. This is not, of course, simply a history lesson: moving assembly lines continue to be used in industrial production throughout the world today.

But at the same time, and it is an important theoretical and practical lesson, this apparent increase in managerial power produced new kinds of power amongst workers (again, an example of an unintended consequence). For now it was possible to bring production to a grinding halt throughout the factory by the simple expedient of stopping production in one place. The familiar phrase 'putting a spanner in the works' derives from this. By dropping (as it might be) a spanner at one point in the conveyor mechanism, the whole line stopped. And, in fact, this kind of sabotage is an enduring feature of Fordist systems. Ford itself managed to implement the system through a combination of offering relatively high wages and operating, especially during the 1920s and 1930s, in a high unemployment era. Nonetheless, not only sabotage but high levels of absenteeism and staff turnover dogged Fordism in similar ways and for similar reasons to the basic Taylorist system.

conclusion

Fordism represents the fullest working out of a particular, massively influential, approach to organizing work. So significant is it that many commentators have spoken of a Fordist era. As Merkle (1980) explains, it spread to all parts of the industrialized world, and its techniques were by no means confined to capitalist societies. On the contrary, Lenin and Stalin both admired Taylor's work and used precisely his techniques to undertake speedy industrialization of the largely agrarian economy of the Soviet Union after the 1917 Russian revolution. That they did so reminds us that, whatever difficulties it faced or created, this approach to organizing allowed unprecedented levels of productivity. And we shouldn't be too moralistic about this: Soviet industrial productivity created the tanks and planes which played a central part in the defeat of Nazi Germany.

And this of course brings us right back to Weber's ideas. His observation that rational-legal, or bureaucratic, organization was taking over was the observation that such organizations were more technically efficient than others. The modern world is the world of efficiency in which the focus is upon the best means to achieve particular ends. The management principles of Taylor and Ford embody just this formal rationality and continue to define, at least partially and perhaps substantially, management to the present day. For, on the one hand, despite some talk to the contrary, it is possible to find organizations all over the world following precisely these principles in industrial settings which Taylor would have immediately recognized as similar to the steel fields of nineteenth-century America. But, on the other hand, even where the settings are less familiar, the basic idea of a rationality of means as the sole focus of managerial concern, the ideology of formal rationality, if you will, has endured.

Weber and Taylor were, of course, very different creatures. Taylor was an architect of this ideology whereas Weber was an observer and, in significant respects, a critic. They therefore appear in organization theory in rather different ways. In conventional, textbook accounts Taylor is seen as a pioneer in the emergence of modern management. The position of Weber is more interesting. His adoption into the 'canon' of organization theory (as opposed to conventional sociology) relied on a very partial reading of his work that ignored his reservations about bureaucracy and elevated his 'ideal type' to the status of a design model, which was not his intention.

In this chapter I have tried to offer a somewhat different overview of these themes to that conventionally presented to students. On the one hand, I have drawn attention to how the ideas of Weber and Taylor inform organization theory, and this in some ways overlaps with conventional accounts. But, on the other hand, I have tried to indicate some difficulties, limitations and complexities which such accounts fail to mention. However, that is not to say that these conventional accounts are unaware of or unconcerned with at least some version of the problems I have alluded to. They are, and in the next chapter I turn to that body of organization theory which purports to rectify the limitations of bureaucracy and scientific management.

notes

1 It still had force in the background, of course: disobey the law and coercion follows.
2 In a high-profile case in Germany in 2001, a man willingly volunteered to be killed and eaten, and even shared the first course – his severed penis, fried – with the man who went on to kill him (BBC, 2003). I think we are on safe ground in saying that most people would consider this bizarre, and it shows, in admittedly extreme form, the limitations of the 'do as you would be done by' approach to ethics.
3 A more challenging issue in relation to agency is the argument that the very idea – usually, of a choosing individual – is itself one specific to modern, especially Western cultures. I buy the argument that agency is socially constructed but, given that it is so constructed, its effects are the same as if it were an essential property of human beings.
4 It is worth saying that in the higher reaches of physics there is reason to think that predictions can affect the physical behaviour of objects – but in the everyday range of experience this is not so.
5 This is also another example of unintended consequences, but of a particular sort as it arises from actions in response to predictions.
6 Its modern-day equivalents might be the still growing heavy industry of China or the call centres of India. Such locations exhibit many of the techniques developed by Taylor but they also share the sense of being places where the world is being re-made.
7 Yes, I know. But most mechanics are male, aren't they?
8 Of course it's relative: there are legal and social controls over drinking, just as there were on work before scientific management.
9 This was true in the USA even before that country's entry into the war in 1917 because US firms were producing arms for the war and there was already a sense that this was a patriotic priority.

2

Human Relations Theory and People Management

The minutiae of the human soul ... emerged as a new domain for management.

Nikolas Rose

Conventional textbooks often set up a simple story about organization theory which has a very appealing structure. In this story, there is a good guy and a bad guy. Who gets to play which role sometimes shifts, but most often the bad guy is the scientific management approach and the good guy is human relations theory. This is a flawed story in my view, and the way I will tell the story emphasizes the many connections and similarities between the two. But I suppose the fact that I am referring to 'the two' implies that there must be some points of difference as well. Maybe so, but it is a different sort of difference to that which standard commentaries identify.

Human relations theory (HRT) is normally thought of as having its roots in the Hawthorne Studies conducted in the 1920s and 1930s at the Hawthorne works of the Western Electric Company, near Chicago in the USA. These studies have now taken on an almost mythological status within the study of organization, so that the details of what happened there and even when they happened are reported differently in different accounts. The grossest example is the way that many students refer to 'Hawthorne' as a person not a place! But even in the academic literature different books give 1923, 1924 and 1927 as the date the studies started and give all kinds of accounts of the research. Related to this mythology is a disjuncture between these precise details of what was done and what was written, and the received version of what HRT is. Since HRT was the work of many years and many people, it contains a huge amount of variation and nuance (some of it extremely interesting) which is not captured by the received version.[1] Although it would certainly be worthwhile to look at the detail (Schwartzman, 1993, is a nice place to start), it is perhaps more important to examine the received version, for it is this which figures most strongly both in textbooks and, consequently, in the way that HRT is used to structure understandings of organizations, especially on the part of their managers. Indeed, as Nancy Harding (2003) observes of the conventional canon of management thinkers:

> ... neither the writers themselves nor indeed what they wrote is important. What defines them as important ... is what they signify, i.e. conventionality, continuity, the conservative way, or, in one word, patriarchy. (2003: 117)

The basic suggestion of the received version of HRT is that through a series of experiments and interviews, the Hawthorne researchers and, most notably, the man who became their chief popularizer and canonical emblem, Elton Mayo, identified the importance of 'the human factor' in organizations. That meant that workers were now recognized as having social needs and interests such that they could no longer be regarded as the economically motivated automatons envisaged by Taylorism.

Within these terms, two parts of the studies stand out as being especially important: the 'illumination experiment' and the 'bank wiring room experiment'. In the first of these, lighting levels were varied up and down within an experimental group of workers, whilst light levels were left unchanged within a control group. Almost all of the lighting changes led to an increase in productivity and, most interesting of all, productivity also increased within the control group. What was going on? Apparently, it was the fact that something 'unusual' was happening and that the workers felt that they were part of it and that what they were doing was of interest and importance to the researchers. It was this that caused the increase in productivity and which demonstrated that the workers could not be regarded as mere parts in the organizational machine. Thus was born the notion of the 'Hawthorne effect', a staple part not just of organization theory but of social science as a whole, the idea that the very fact of observing human behaviour had an influence upon that behaviour. This, by the way, is just another aspect of what I said in the last chapter about the way that, since human beings have agency, they respond to how they are treated, to predictions made about them and, in this case, to being studied in ways which are not true of inanimate objects.

The other study I will mention is that conducted in the bank wiring room. Here, a small group of male workers were engaged in producing electrical components. It emerged that the group set informal norms around production levels so that, rather than produce their maximum output (which would earn them a bonus), the workers performed sub-optimally. These norms were enforced by a mixture of peer pressure (including the physical sanction of 'pinging' which sounds innocuous but meant being hit on the leg with an iron bar) and an unofficial 'gang leader'. This suggested that workers were not solely motivated by economic considerations and, moreover, that the 'informal side of the organization' was as important as, or maybe even more important than, the formal side (i.e. the rules and official hierarchy).

The discovery of the human factor, so the story goes, ushered in a new era in which workers' needs were acknowledged and met. This claim fits not just the 'good guy, bad guy' story, it also promotes a version of organization theory as gradually discovering and refining truths, much in the way that science is supposed to proceed. There is one tiny flaw in all this, however: it's not true. It's not true for lots of reasons. One is that an interest in workers going beyond economic concerns can be found well before the Hawthorne studies. It was present in the various attempts by nineteenth-century industrialists, especially those of Quaker background, to meet the 'moral needs' of workers. This is evidenced by towns like Port Sunlight and Bourneville in the UK, where housing and religious and communal activities were designed to cater for workers' leisure time and to provide an environment conducive to good living. True, it was the new 'science' of psychology rather than paternalistic religiosity that informed HRT but they share a similar humanizing imperative, and the latter had a paternalism of its own.

The second issue is that the original impetus for the Hawthorne experiments was firmly located within the tradition of scientific management, well established by the 1920s. The desire to ascertain the effect of lighting levels on productivity was informed by the idea that management was about the control of physical variables, and in fact there were many other experiments designed to explore a whole array of such variables.

Finally, and crucially, it is simply wrong to think that Taylor had been unaware of, or was uninterested in, the 'informal side' of the organization. On the contrary, the heart of Taylor's project was an attempt to *overcome* its effects. For the output restrictions observed in the bank wiring room were nothing other than an instance of what Taylor had called the 'systematic soldiering' of the workforce. That is not to say that his approach was the same as HRT; it was not. For whereas Taylor sought to eradicate the informal side of the organization, the human relations message was to acknowledge its irrepressibility and to find ways of managing it into an alignment with the formal parts and purposes of the organization.

And so now HRT begins to take on a very different aspect. In one way it is a response to the failure, or at least limitations, of scientific management as a means of organizational control. But it is a response which in many ways offers not an alternative to, but an extension of, scientific management. What I mean to say is that HRT bears the same footprint of formal or instrumental rationality as that which is to be found in scientific management. My former colleague John Roberts wrote a highly illuminating case study around this theme many years ago (Roberts, 1984). He contrasts the approaches of 'Dave' and 'Val' to managing their teams of telesales workers. Dave is a scientific management type of manager, who tries to avoid any human contact with his staff and treats them as economically motivated automatons. Val takes a more human relations type of approach. She tries to understand the problems and anxieties of her staff and to encourage their wider motivations to work. But – and this is the crucial point – they both sought to control their teams: one by *avoiding* human relationships and one *through* human relationships.

If this is right, then the difference between scientific management and HRT is a 'tactical' one. That's a real difference, and it would be crass to deny it, not least because the two tactics create different working environments which will be experienced as such by people within them. But it would also be crass to romanticize that difference. For how will Dave and Val be judged, by others and, perhaps, themselves? According to the extent to which their approaches yield higher or lower sales. This is why they are both instrumentally rational versions of organization.

Why, then, does the received version of HRT fight shy of acknowledging its commonality with scientific management? I think there are two reasons for this. One is straightforward and relates to some specific difficulties faced by management as an occupation or even, aspirationally, a profession. The other is much more complicated and is to do with the idea of 'humanism'.

Later in this chapter I will talk quite a bit about management as an occupation. But what I want to say here is that the establishment of it as a respectable, let alone respected, activity was by no means straightforward. Today, we live in a world where to be a manager is, in many people's eyes, to be recognized as a person of some consequence (though this may be changing, as I will discuss in Chapter 5). But this was not always so. In the early nineteenth century, the term 'manager' was regarded with some suspicion, much as we might use the word 'cowboy' or 'scammer' today. As I mentioned in the last chapter, the new breed of scientific managers were also accused of undermining individual initiative and freedom. By the twentieth century, managers were much better established, but the legacy of scientific management with its conflicts and inhumane efficiency hardly made it a prestigious label. Satirized and derided in films like Charlie Chaplin's *Modern Times* and novels like Aldous Huxley's *Brave New World*, management had an image problem in the 1920s and 1930s. It's not hard to see why. Imagine a manager going home and being questioned by his (for most managers of the day were men) child:

Child: What do you do all day, Dad?
Dad: Well, I, sort of, exploit people.
Child: How do you mean?
Dad: Well, you know, I dehumanize them by making them work as
         hard as I can for as little money as possible.
Child: Oh.

It was embarrassing stuff. A much better picture was offered by HRT. Management could now be reconfigured as an altogether more humane undertaking which ameliorated rather than inflamed social conflict and, perhaps most important of all, was about 'helping' rather than exploiting the worker. This latter point came out of the tendency of Mayo, in particular, to conceptualize worker resistance as a psychological maladjustment rather than a rational response to conditions of employment. Famously, or infamously, Mayo went so far as to propose that membership of a trade union was a sign of mental illness. In fact, in this respect, Taylor's writings show much more empathy with workers' experiences than those of Mayo. Taylor after all had worked as a machine operator, and he did not find worker recalcitrance particularly objectionable at a personal level, albeit that he wanted to overcome it. But that overcoming presented management as, nakedly, being about power. Mayo's less sympathetic account of worker resistance paradoxically cast the manager as assisting the worker to make a normal adjustment to factory life.

So now a different conversation becomes possible:

Child: What do you do all day, Dad?
Dad: Well, I, sort of, help people.
Child: How do you mean?
Dad: Well, you know, if they feel unhappy at work I make them see
         that I care about them and that it's not so bad.
Child: Oh, Dad. That's great.

We probably shouldn't discount the fact that being able to give a positive sounding account of one's work to family and friends might persuade managers to embrace HRT. But, in any case, there were wider constituencies to whom, in a less naïve way, a similar account could helpfully be given. In a society[2] racked by social and industrial conflict, and extremely fearful that such conflict might lead to an emulation of the 1917 Russian Revolution, managers really needed to present a more humane and less confrontational face than they had hitherto been able to do. And there was more at stake here than the manipulation of image. It was also the case that the scientific management system had indeed thrown up new problems – sabotage, poor quality, high staff turnover, absenteeism – to which the human relations approach might offer a solution. 'Technical' and 'ideological' factors are never separable: they reinforce each other.

All of this is fairly easy to understand. What is perhaps less clear is the more general question of the place of humanism within Western societies, of which HRT management is but one, specific, manifestation. There is so much that could be said about this that I hesitate to plunge in, but it is necessary for me to do so because it is not possible to understand organization without seeing how it stands in this wider context.[3]

what is it to be human?

Part of what has made modern societies modern is a move away from traditional belief systems in which the social order was simply preordained by the will of God. The eighteenth-century Enlightenment had broken down much of this reasoning – for example, the belief that kings ruled by divine right – and, as mentioned in the last chapter, had substituted the idea that individuals could use their own reason rather than rely upon the received authority of others. Clearly Weber's charting of the rise of rational-legal, as against traditional, authority and of the development of the bureaucratic organization, was part of the same flow of thought. But if individuals, rather than God or his representatives in the Church or the Monarchy, were now at the centre of things – who were these individuals? There were many takes on this question, but they crystallized around the idea of autonomous human beings, complete and sufficient in themselves, capable of rationality, capable of choice, capable of moral conduct and, by virtue of all possessing these traits, all entitled to certain rights.

So we find, from the Enlightenment onwards, the understanding that people had the right to be treated in certain ways. This led to all kinds of reforms, including the ideas that people could (with certain restrictions such as, until the twentieth century, being male) have a say in who governed them; have a fair trial; speak their opinions without punishment; own their own property; be equal in the eyes of the law and so on. These are all very familiar things. It is easy to see how central such ideas are to modern forms of organization. When we think of a worker agreeing to work in exchange for a certain sum of money, we are presupposing a

whole series of choices and rights. It is a bizarre thought that, for someone of my age, some didn't always apply to my grandmother and almost
none to my great-great-great grandfather and of course many don't apply
to men and women in various countries today. This should alert us to
the historical and cultural mutability of the idea of 'personhood' – or,
what a human being is. Who knows what it will mean for our great-
great-great grandchildren, or even for our children?[4]

This idea of personhood substantially deepened in the twentieth century. It moved from a philosophical, political or legal notion to a much
more embodied or personalized one. If eighteenth and nineteenth centuries had established some ideas about economic and political personhood (or at least, as I have suggested, manhood), then the twentieth
century extended this into the psychological sphere. The intellectual
revolution associated with Freud (but, as with Taylor, no less attributable to others) established human beings as no mere conscious decision-
making machines but as possessors of an unconscious and of all of the
complexities of neurosis, motivation, desire and so on that map us out
as human in our present-day understanding of that term. The 'I' had
been given depth, so that we learned to understand our real selves as a
complex, multi-layered thing, understandable only partially to ourselves but perhaps accessible through the expertise of a psychoanalyst.
'Subconsciously', someone might say, 'I think that what attracted me to
my husband was the way he's an authority figure, a bit like my father'.
It is a surprising thought that no one could have said such a thing, or
have been understood if they had said it, as little as 120 years ago.

And, of course, at the same time that all this was going on, there was
also a steady but sure erosion of the religious belief which had been the
dominant way of understanding the self and its relationship with the
wider world for several centuries, in its Christian form, and perhaps for
all of history in one form or another. To be sure that change has happened slowly and, for a great many people, not at all. But, where it did,
it placed the individual at the centre of the universe. It suggested that
people – and perhaps society – were not just important but that they
were all that there was. Life ended with death, and the authority of God
was replaced either by the authority of society, most likely in the form
of the State, or by no more than the individual pursuit of desire and
pleasure. It is easy to see that all of the main currents of Western society
in, say, the last century have been concerned in making sense of this:
Fascism, Communism, Existentialism, Hippie Culture, Neo-liberalism
and our present culture of individualistic consumption of material goods
are all examples.

Did any of this add up to a better, more accurate picture of personhood or the relation of people one to another? That really seems like an

impossible question to answer. I suppose that from a religious perspective there would be some answers (mainly negative), but then adherence to a religion might be seen as no more than a dogmatic response to the very question posed by the dissolution of certainty. I think that since the picture we currently have of personhood is so very different to that held even a relatively short time ago, then it is likely that the future will have a different picture and that therefore it would be foolish to give undue weight to our present picture. What is certain is that modern understandings of the human being have had dramatic effects upon how we live, upon art, culture, politics – upon everything that human beings do.

And that, of course, includes organizations. How could it not? The puzzling thing is that these kinds of themes and discussions are so absent from most of the organization theory textbooks. How can it be that they just assume that the way things are round about now is some kind of immutable, stable truth?[5] I suspect that many organization theorists would say that all the themes I have alluded to (in the most cursory way) are about 'something else' – politics, philosophy, society – but that is manifestly nonsense. How could organizations possibly be abstracted from these?

Returning to HRT, it seems clear to me that its appeal, its very emergence, fitted into this shifting understanding of personhood like, to use a clichéd term, a hand in a glove. The invocation of 'humanity' is one obvious clue to this. For HRT engaged directly with emerging understandings about the 'depth' of personhood. It suggested that 'beneath' the economic motivations of Taylorist workers lay some more profound realities, realities which it took a very specialized kind of manager to understand (another reason why we should give managers respect, then). But understanding was only one part of the picture. Much more important, as for the psychoanalysts, was 'adjustment'. The new domain of the psyche was also a domain in which problems occurred and had to be dealt with. The self was no longer something just to be taken at face value, but was a terrain of worry.

That worry was both social – the problems of criminality, madness, delinquency, alcoholism, perversion and so on – and individual. Individuals, along with their autonomy, their rights, their choices, had acquired responsibilities and anxieties. Freedom, in Erich Fromm's haunting (1942) phrase, had brought the 'fear of freedom'. You can see exactly the same thing today, in very advanced form. On the one hand, there is an ever greater array of social worries about what people do with their freedom – molest children, plant bombs, take drugs. On the other hand, there is huge individual insecurity – am I earning enough, good in bed, living a healthy lifestyle? Am I too fat, too much in debt, getting good enough grades?

All this is to say that a new terrain opened up, in organizations at least as much as elsewhere, into which management could now be inserted. This, I think, is the real significance of the Hawthorne Studies. They legitimated a new managerial arena. At one level it could be read as an imposition. Management was no longer concerned with what workers did – with, if you will, the body – but with what people are. Worker hopes, fears, motivations, anxieties, aspirations all fell into the locus of management. One reading of this would be to see organizations as becoming ever-more intrusive. The private, non-work sphere gets progressively more eroded. For these new understandings of work began to break down the dividing line between work and the real, true self. I mean: under scientific management systems it might be possible to say that your real self was what lay outside work – your family, friends, hobbies or whatever. But HRT begins (although less dramatically than some of its successors, as discussed in the next chapter) to say that that distinction is false.

However, if my earlier idea about the changing nature of personhood is correct, then it follows that neither the claim that the real self lies outside of work nor the claim that it lies inside of work can be sustained. All we can say is that, at various times, different apprehensions of personhood hold good. So isn't it more to the point to say not that HRT invaded the territory of the private self but that it actually contributed to mapping the territory out as one to be either left alone or invaded, by contributing to defining private and public selves? For it tells us that the human being is always, unavoidably, present at work. This has profound consequences for organizations, but it is also highly significant for individuals. If modernity left a pervasive void of meaning and a pervasive insecurity about identity, then work now stood ready to provide meaning and identity. After all, what is one of the first things we say when we meet a new person? We might start by asking their name, and then, perhaps, where they come from. But very soon we will ask: what do you do?

Once work begins to express and define who we are (and in the process of doing so, to close certain things down as to what we are *not*), a whole new set of concerns becomes manifest in organizations. Once HRT had entered the world of organizations and organization theorists, a whole edifice of knowledge about people at work was gradually elaborated. Such knowledge is the staple of the conventional study of organizations and includes such things as personality type, motivation and job satisfaction, group dynamics, leadership and much more. It is tempting to see these as more or less descriptive accounts of people at work, but this is wrong for two reasons. The first is an extension of what I have already tried to say. There is no ultimate description of people but rather ascriptions which, if believed and enforced, are taken as descriptions – they constitute or construct reality. For example, is the difference between a child and an adult a real difference, or is it rather that where we draw the line and enforce it (for example, by conferring certain rights at particular ages) takes on the appearance of a real difference? We could say that people divide into those who are right-handed and those who are left-handed and confer different rights on them, but we don't. On the other hand, we can and do say that people divide into male and female and, in many societies, confer different rights accordingly. Or we divide people into different nationalities and confer different rights accordingly. These things are a matter of what is socially agreed and also of power – who has the power to draw the distinctions and to enforce the effects of these distinctions.

So when personality types are divided into, say, introvert and extrovert, or any of the many other variations on this theme in organization theory, and when on the basis of this ascription decisions are made about who to employ and who not to employ, then exactly the same processes of distinction making and enforcement are present. The legacy of HRT has been to multiply these schema for making distinctions between people, and you can see in any organization theory textbook an endless array of models, typologies, 2-by-2 matrices and so on which replicate these distinctions but treat them as descriptions rather than ascriptions – as being rooted in a self-evident truth rather than being the outcome of a social process. In this way, organization theory is a part of making this social process happen. So, to take some well-known examples: the distinctions Maslow draws between different motivators; or Herzberg's distinction of motivators and hygiene factors; or the distinction of task and role orientation in management style; or McGregor's theory X and theory Y – all these serve to constitute or construct the organizational world and do not simply describe it.

Now, undoubtedly, the drawing of distinctions is almost unavoidable if we are to make any kind of sense of the world around us, including that of organizations (even to speak of 'the world around us' is to make a distinction). And it is not the case that this began in organization theory with HRT. After all, scientific management draws all kinds of distinctions between efficiency and inefficiency, for example. However, because HRT draws the 'whole person' into the organizational ambit, the impact of all of these supposedly descriptive distinctions is potentially much greater. The stakes are very high when we think about organizations, just because work is such a central part of society; but the stakes get even higher when work organizations and personhood become inextricably linked. And this means that those of us who study organizations, and the much larger number of us who work in them, need to be much more sceptical than organization theory normally encourages us to be.

The constitutive or constructive nature of organization theory is one reason why we have to be cautious about the way we use its concepts to think about people in organizations. But there is a second issue, and this relates to the continuities between HRT and scientific management which I pointed to earlier. For not only does organization theory contribute to constituting what it claims to be describing, but it does so in particular ways, for particular reasons. The impetus for HRT was that of organizational control and, more particularly, the attempt by managers to gain control over organizational processes. So the kind of knowledge produced and the uses to which it is put have to be read in the light of that aspiration for control. Organization theory is often, and certainly in the case of HRT, indistinguishable from theories of managing. Organization theorists have often been, to use Baritz's evocative (1960) phrase, 'servants of power'. That may or may not be a good thing (I think it is a bad thing), but it must mean that organization theory has to be read with an eye to the purposes it serves, which means giving more attention to management than I have so far done.

the rise and rise of management

Management has been one of the great success stories of the modern world. As many writers have remarked – so many that it has almost become clichéd – the etymological origins of management lie in two terms – the French *menager* and the Italian *maneggiare* – the first denoting domestic or household organization, the second the handling of horses. The ultimate origin lies in the Latin word *manus* or hand. What this may be taken to point to (if you will forgive the pun) is the essentially humble and mundane meaning of management, the sense that it is something dispersed, done by everyone. This sense is recalled when we say something like 'I managed to catch the bus on time' or 'I managed to avoid arguing with him'.

But although we do use the word manage in that way, that isn't what we usually think of when we talk about management, and it certainly isn't the kind of thing with which 'management schools' and management studies are normally concerned. They configure management in an altogether more grandiose way. But what is management? There is no straightforward answer to that question, and the problem is not one of definition. It is not that there is some 'thing' – management – to be described and, in being described, delineated from all sorts of other 'things'. As with personhood, what is at stake is a social construction in which competing claims are made about management and, at different times and by different audiences, are accepted. A good illustration of this is found in a study of management which has received far less attention than it deserves:

> I was styled a 'manager' and my wife ... was a 'housewife'. I can remember well the blessed relief of leaving my house and its attendant chaos each morning to go off to my oh-so-demanding 'management' job. In what sense ... was my wife not 'managing' and in what sense was my work ... more essentially managerial than hers? At work I had another woman to make sure I managed properly ... This one wasn't styled a manager either, but the same essential question held good for her; in what sense is the work of a secretary not managerial? (Mant, 1977: 1)

I think that Mant's questions in this passage do two things. One is to remind us that management carries the embedded meaning of the daily accomplishment of life's 'business'. The other is that the way the line gets drawn between managers and others is an accomplishment of power. Some kinds of claims to be a manager don't register, and if they are brought to our attention the response is: 'yeah, of course'. Other kinds of claims jar, and invite the response: 'oh yeah?'. So it's really no great surprise that the two people Mant identifies as being engaged in managerial roles without being awarded the title of manager are women – his wife and his secretary. *Their* kind of management is just boring old house management ('oh yeah?'). *Real* management is what the guys do, with spreadsheets and strategies and meetings and budgets. It's what managers do ('yeah, of course').

So, sometimes, management seems to mean a group of people – managers. In this way we may talk about 'the management', and mean, usually, a group distinct from 'the workers'. What makes them managers? Well, one important answer might be just that they are called managers. I'll come back to this, but one thing which is notable about present day organizations is how the title of manager has become something of a debased currency, so that what was once a loo cleaner might now be glossed as a facilities inspection and hygiene manager. This is interesting because it points to the mutability of the status of managers. Over the last one hundred years or more, and especially in the last few decades, we've got used to the idea of managers being fairly high status, in a desirable career option, respected and well-paid. But as I mentioned earlier this wasn't always the case, and perhaps is ceasing to be so, as discussed in Chapter 5, so management had to go through a long process of what would nowadays be called 'image-building'. That process was ultimately successful, though:

> Management will remain a basic and dominant institution perhaps as long as Western civilization itself survives. (Drucker, 1955: 1)

This is heady stuff. To go from horse-handling to bulwark of civilization in the space of about a century is no mean achievement, and if the tone of Drucker's eulogy is rather breathless it does no more than sum up what many others said and believed. Note that he is not talking about managers per se, but about management as an 'institution'. No doubt there is some overlap between the two, but the point is that it renders management as something more than 'the management'. How did management achieve this position? Analysts are divided between at least three competing explanations, which I have outlined elsewhere (Grey, 1999). First, there is a 'technical' explanation – that management arose to solve the functional problems of large-scale organization. Second, there is an 'elite' explanation – that management arose to define and defend the interests of a particular group, namely managers. Third, there is a 'political' explanation – that management arose in order to control and discipline workers.

Earlier I talked about the struggles that management engaged in to make itself legitimate in the eyes of society. These took two forms, of which one was a kind of technical justification – that management made things more efficient; and the other a more ideological justification – that management helped to make things more humane. Of course these are not really separate so much as reinforcing justifications: scientific management had as part of its pitch a fair division of labour and a fair reward, whilst human relations approaches have always claimed, even if they have been unable to prove it, that workers who are managed humanely are also more productive. In this sense, HRT is about humanization as technique.

Looked at in this way, it is easy to see the relationship between technical and elite views of management. If management is a technical necessity, arising from the functional requirements for efficiency in large-scale enterprises, then this makes out a strong case for the elite status of managers. A much stronger case than, for example, a bald demand for status, power and money. That may be what drives the elite explanation, but for it to work it has to be translated into terms with a greater legitimacy, and the two-pronged claims (technical and ideological) within the case for management do just that.

Of course, someone might object to this by saying that what is important is that it is true that management fulfils a technical necessity, and
because it is true then managers came to form an elite group. All my talk
of legitimation is beside the point. Against this, I could point to the argument that management is really about control, not technical necessity.
My imaginary heckler might then say that this too misses the point since
it is precisely the delivery of control – whether delivered through hard
systems or soft soap – which constitutes the technical necessity of management. But now I have a good put-down line, which is that it is highly
questionable whether management does in fact deliver such control,
even accepting that this is its aim, because of the issues of resistance and
unintended consequences I rehearsed in the first chapter; the idea that
management is a perennially failing operation. And if my 'theoretical'
arguments on this aren't acceptable, then just consider the fact that,
despite well over a century of trying to find the answers to managerial
problems, it remains the case that organizations are continually chasing
new solutions and new approaches – and the job of management appears
never to be done.

So, at the very least, the truth of the technical necessity for management is endlessly debatable and requires the continual advancement of
claims which may or may not be accepted by particular people at particular times. It is therefore quite sensible to look at the way those claims
are advanced. And here I think we have to go into deeper water than
simply talking about their content towards considering what it is that
makes them, at least potentially, plausible.

management and modernism

It is no coincidence that Peter Drucker talked about management's
dominance in the context of Western civilization. Earlier I talked about
modern understandings of personhood and the way that the breakdown
of religious belief brought with it a new accent upon the individual. But
alongside and in various ways linked to that came another development.
If the world and what happened in it was no longer thought of in terms
of the will and design of God, it became possible to think of that world
instead as something that could be ordered according to the will and design
of people. Social organization ceases to be preordained but becomes an
arena for intervention and control.

Control is perhaps a key term here. The emergence of experimental
natural science and the growing body of theory that went with it, which
quickened from the seventeenth century onwards, yielded the possibility
of control over the physical circumstances of life. In its wake came a huge

array of new technologies – from medicine to energy generation – which fundamentally altered the relationship between human beings and nature. But if the physical world could be controlled in this way, then why should social organization be any different? It is from this basic question that, amongst other things, the positivism I discussed in the Introduction emerged. For at heart, positivism is the attempt to apply the same reasoning to social phenomena as had been introduced to the physical realm.

Obviously the attempt to control social organization was not confined to the modern world that emerged from the scientific revolution. Rulers of all kinds have always sought, and often achieved, control over people, territories, money and so on. What was different, though, was the idea that this could be done systematically through the development and application of the new bodies of knowledge which emerge in the modern era – statistics, economics and sociology being some of the more obvious examples. To design society as if it were a machine, running according to rules which were fully understood and demonstrated – that was the dream. And it is easy to see that this dovetails with Weber's observations about the rise of the bureaucratic organization, for what was this other than a rule-based social machine?

It should not be thought that this search for control was animated solely by a drive for power, and again in this way it perhaps differs from other, pre-modern attempts at control. For along with the search for control was a strong ideology of progress. Just as the natural world could be controlled for the better – for a healthier, more comfortable and richer life – so social life could be controlled in order to yield improvements. Society could become more educated, more knowledgeable, more civilized and cultured (even 'society' conceived of as an object of analysis and a defined arena of behaviour is part of this modern revolution). This of course did require control, for it meant purging ignorance and bad behaviour. Perhaps this too could be thought of as an intervention in nature. Human beings might be naturally corrupt and vicious, just as mountains were naturally difficult to cross. But if you could build roads to cross mountains, then why couldn't you build institutions to improve humanity?

Management is interesting to me because it precisely traverses these twin tracks of modern thought – the systematic control of nature and the systematic control of society. For if the revolution in natural science made possible the steam engines and precision engineering of the factory, then the revolution in social science lent itself to attempts to control the factory workers. Or, to put it differently and perhaps rather better, there is no sharp distinction to be drawn in the modern world between the natural and social domains. Both, as Ian Hacking (1983) has it, become arenas which can be 'represented' and 'intervened' in.

What that distinction points to goes beyond what I have said so far, and is worth pausing to consider.

At one level, and I think it is the one that we normally think of, when we think of such things at all, the modern world represents no more than the discovery of ways of intervening. That is, the dumb world was just sitting there, ready and waiting to have things done to it once people got round to working out how to do them. When they did, modernity got going. But this misses a crucial part of what happened. Before intervention could really begin there needed to be a new way of thinking about, and knowing, the world – a way of representing it. That wasn't about discovering new things, so much as 're-presenting' old things in a new way. Was poverty part of the ordained world of God? Or was it because poor people were lazy? Or was it because rich people had grabbed all the wealth? Represent it the first way and intervention is at best pointless and at worse sinful. Represent it in one of the other ways, and intervention becomes possible. More than that, it calls forth a multiplication of representations, for example drawing the boundary between rich and poor and collecting statistics on how many people are poor, where they live and how they live. So now representation is both a new way of thinking and a new way of knowing. And it is a 'problem' to be dealt with or intervened in – perhaps by punishing the poor for their laziness, perhaps by castigating the rich for their greed, depending upon how the representation was effected.

A similar example, which I talked about earlier, is the constitutive role of organization theory with its distinctions and categories. But now I am talking about something more fundamental than organization theory: the very basic parameters of how modern views of the world operate. Now it is of course the case that this can be discussed in much more sophisticated ways than I have done here, and a host of social theorists and philosophers have done just that, but I am not going to do so. One reason is just my own ignorance. But this necessity can become a virtue for the following reason. The camp followers of modernity, which includes most of the readers of this book as well as myself, don't operate with any very sophisticated grasp of their world, any more than medieval peasants were any great shakes at theology. But a received wisdom, a folk-wisdom almost, informs our thoughts and actions and, in particular, it informs the theory and practice of management. My concern is to show that this received wisdom is not just 'the way things are' but that it marks management out as being embedded in a particular, historically bounded and philosophically informed, view of the world; the details of that history and philosophy I leave to those who are better qualified to discuss it.

For it must be obvious that management is all of a piece with this representation and intervention which I have talked about. At the most basic level, management assumes manageability – that the world can be known and operated upon, and these terms are virtually interchangeable with representation and intervention. In this sense management is something which literally could not have existed, and does not exist, outside of modernity. But, beyond that, management consists of a distinctive series of often extremely complex ways of effecting representations and conducting interventions. For example, consider a workshop in which ten people are making, I don't know, tables. How can it be represented?

We could make a literal representation by drawing a picture, but that wouldn't be a distinctive 'management' representation because it wouldn't (or at least not obviously) allow any kind of managerial intervention. However, if we represented it as a series of inputs and outputs; or as an array of costs and incomes; or as a series of bundles of wants and needs (of customers, workers, etc.), then this would be a management representation. It might take the form of a flow chart, a set of accounts or a treatise on marketing or personnel psychology. These are all management representations and they all allow managerial interventions, such as redesign of resource flows; cutting of costs; advertising campaigns to customers or motivation programmes for workers.

So, now, let's go back to managers. If I am right (something which can by no means be taken for granted), then there is something more fundamental at stake than the technical, elite and political explanations for its emergence and functioning, even though it has a bearing upon these explanations. Managers are bearers of a particular kind of expertise – the capacity to represent and intervene in particular ways. But these ways are arbitrary and they are contested. They are arbitrary because it is impossible to say that representing the workshop as a balance sheet is more true to reality than painting the scene on a canvas. And because they are arbitrary they must be contestable, in the sense that it is always possible to say that a different representation should be made. This contestability is evident both within management (for example, between an accounting or a human psychology representation) and from without. For, apart from the possibility of representing the workshop in different managerial ways, it is also possible to represent it as, say, a place of exploitation, power and conflict.

I'm going to bring back my imaginary heckler, who might say that I have done no more than state – at excruciating length and in pompous ways – that management is what managers do. Well, maybe that's a fair comment, but I think I've done something a bit more than that. One thing is that I've hopefully shown at a fundamental level what it is that managers do when they manage: they don't just 'get things done'; they represent and intervene in particular ways. That might (perhaps) be interesting in itself, but it also helps to explain the way that these managers are hostages or, if you prefer, emblems of a particular way of looking at the world; itself no more valid and no more enduring than any other. As the Peter Drucker quote suggests, by the middle of the twentieth century, this way of looking at the world was very much in the ascendant. That this was so was in no small part due to the combination of HRT with its supposed opposite in bureaucratic and scientific management approaches to organizations. For taken together these provided the technical and ideological justification for the managerial way of representing and intervening in the realm of organizations.

By welding these things together, it is possible to see how the rise of management is inseparable from the rise of *people* management, or to use what for many years was the preferred term 'man management',[6] which grew out of HRT. It is emphatically not the case that other kinds of management (for example, scientific management) were unconcerned with such people management and, indeed, it is impossible to see how it could be. But HRT filled out and made explicit just how extensive was the ambit of management in the modern world. It is no coincidence that the commonest definition of management is given in terms of 'getting things done through other people'. It is a revealing definition in the central role it places on people in management, the instrumentality of the way it apprehends people and its scope. For what are the 'things' that can be got done in this way? Why, anything and everything.

conclusion

The classical issues in the study of organizations with which the first two chapters of this book have been concerned both reflected and contributed to building a powerful and influential edifice. This edifice presents it as self-evident that we live in an organizational world – and, moreover, an organizational world of a particular, managerial sort. The significance of this is not, primarily, the rise of an elite group of managers but rather the rise of a managerial understanding of the organizational world. I stress this because such a view is relatively detached from the fate of managers as an occupational group. As I will explore in later chapters, an increasing accent upon self-management relies upon this managerial apprehension even when it also threatens the position of managers as such.

It is normal when studying organizations as part of a management degree to understand things like bureaucratic theory, scientific management, HRT and management generally as entirely unproblematic. They may sometimes be presented as dated (albeit foundational), but to do so does not challenge the way that they take the managerial representation of the organizational world as if it is the only representation (as if, in fact, it is simply reality). The account I have offered is rather different. I suggest that the orthodox story is a construction which conveniently excludes almost everything of importance. First and foremost, it excludes the way that it *is* a construction. Related to that, it also fails to understand how organization theory is part and parcel of a particular philosophical and historical context. And related to *this*, it fails to acknowledge the ways that organization theory provides a technical and ideological legitimation of management, rather than simply the description of organizational life it purports to be. Finally, by a relentless focus on a one-sided picture of instrumental rationality and control – whether overtly or, as with human relations approaches, covertly – it fails to understand the severe limitations, both in principle and practice, of this picture.

Defective as this picture may be, it is the one that has been taken forward into the contemporary study and practice of organizations with which the next three chapters of this book are concerned. And its significance is wider than the study of 'people in organizations'. Nowadays management courses virtually always fall into three kinds of components. One is explicitly concerned with, precisely, people and is found in modules on organizations, human resource management or some variant of these. A second consists of modules in things like strategy or marketing which usually adopt some quasi-economic model of people as, for example, rational consumers (in other words, bad social science). The third is concerned with management 'science' – operations, finance and so on. This component normally treats 'people' by ignoring them in favour of some fantasy about organizations in which human beings are just removed (which, ironically, just means bad science as well as bad social science). The fact is that all management subjects carry within them assumptions and theories about people. The issue is how explicitly and, when made explicit, how adequately. Subjects like marketing and finance are as much about 'people' as organizational behaviour – they are just not very explicit or adequate about it. But mainstream courses in organizations are not much better, treating human beings as a recalcitrant but potentially manageable resource – the 'human resource' as we say nowadays. Indeed the idea of harnessing this resource in ever-more inventive and subtle ways has been at the heart of almost all thinking about management and organizations in recent times, as the next chapter explores.

notes

1   This same disjuncture is present in relation to Taylor's work (and scholarly commentaries on it) and that of many other organizational theorists. It isn't a matter of saying that the received version is deficient in detail or scholarship. They are different things for different purposes. Apart from anything else, received versions are simpler and more memorable. In many ways my purpose in this book is to put out another version of organization theory, no more scholarly than the received version but hopefully no less memorable.

2   I mean Britain, the USA and other industrialized countries between the two World Wars.

3   In the pages which follow I am glossing a fairly freeform version of 'post-structuralism'. It would disrupt my purposes to elaborate this but see, for example, Burrell (1988), Rose (1989) and Hacking (1991) for some of the work which has informed my account.

4   Consider, for example, the possible impact of developments in genetic science and technology for how we come to conceive of personhood in the future. Or how technologies like Facebook have recast the way we understand the public and private self.

5   This is particularly weird given the way that most current texts emphasize how rapid is 'change' in organizations and their world. But change in that kind of thought is only considered in the most limited of ways. See Chapter 4.

6   This usage now seems quaint but is by no means an historical curio. For one of the pervasive biases of organization theory, both mainstream and critical, has been to assume that male experience encapsulates experience in general and that 'man' is equivalent to 'human'. This is a very particular, and particularly important, instance of what I was talking about earlier in terms of the construction of meaning about what it is to be human: specifically, a gendered construction. See Harding (2003).

3

Organizational Culture and Self-Management

It's often safer to be in chains than to be free.

Franz Kafka

In 1982, my main preoccupation was with my first 'serious' girlfriend and, when that preoccupation allowed, with attempts to prepare for my forthcoming A-level exams. I hope that this background will both explain and forgive the fact that I was at the time completely unaware of what I consider to be a truly awful book that was published that year. With intellectual roots which recognizably went back to human relations theory (HRT), it and its derivatives continue to transform organizations to the present day. The book, which I think still remains the bestselling management book of all time, was *In Search of Excellence* (Peters and Waterman, 1982).

If it was so awful – trite, bombastic, sloppily researched – how come it was so influential? There are many answers to that but perhaps the most obvious is that, like scientific management and human relations, it chimed with the context of its times. North America had, since the end of the war, been the dominant industrial economy in the world but by the late 1970s had come increasingly under threat, especially from competition from Japan in industries like car and consumer goods manufacture, as well as from other emergent 'tiger economies' in South-East Asia. Indeed, a book by colleagues of Peters and Waterman at the management consultants McKinsey & Co, published that same year, had proclaimed the need for US companies to embrace the 'art of Japanese management' (Pascale and Athos, 1982).

Pascale and Athos proposed that American management had been preoccupied with the rational and systemic aspects of management, like organizational structures and strategies. Japanese companies, they said, had a more holistic approach which included attention to soft and irrational factors – people's skills and management styles. Above all, they said, the Japanese focused on the generation of 'shared values'. Shared values meant that everyone in the organization was committed to common goals such as high-quality output and customer service. As a result, there was less internal conflict, more efficient and effective production, and a high degree of motivation and commitment from everyone in the workplace.[1]

It was very much these kinds of shared values which Peters and Waterman identified as being the culture of excellence which obtained within some of America's top-performing companies. The way forward, then, was for all companies to develop a set of shared values – a strong, or homogeneous, culture – which would then ensure success. And the news was even better. Because values were shared, organizations no longer needed to maintain large hierarchies of managers overseeing the workforce and enforcing the complicated rules of bureaucracy. The workforce would be empowered and, because of its commitment to the culture of excellence, would use its power wisely and for the benefit of the organization. So it would be possible to massively reduce the number of managerial employees and save a great deal of money as a result.

So you could have better products, less waste, less conflict, better service, a happier and fairer workplace and save money into the bargain – if you could just get the culture right. Unfortunately it proved to be a big 'if'. This confident, even utopian, vision of the future has the appearance of optimism, but it was bred of something less cheerful. Apart from increased competition from Asia, the USA continued to bear the scars of the Vietnam and Cambodia wars and to suffer from the effects of the oil price rises of the mid-1970s. It is not fanciful to see culture management ideas as being a response to what was becoming a pervasive crisis of confidence. At all events, it represented part of what the historian Robert Locke (1996) has incisively identified as the 'collapse of the American management mystique'.

The mystique of American management was born out of American military success in the Second World War. The landings in Normandy, in particular, represented a huge logistical achievement, and it was these logistics which were thought to characterize the superiority of American management. However, whilst not denying the significance of the American war effort, nor the huge sacrifices made in the Normandy landings, it is also the case that an important, and perhaps overriding, reason for the victory in Western Europe was that the cream of the German army had been defeated by the Soviet Union on the Eastern front where an estimated 20 million Soviet soldiers and civilians died. Without rehearsing these issues in detail, suffice to say that it is far from clear that American logistics were as central to their military success as had been believed in the immediate post-war period.

There were some other strands of American culture which helped to explain the popularity of the culture approach. America had been in the vanguard of the youthful counter-culture which emerged, especially on the West coast, in the 1960s. Those involved or influenced by it were, by the early 1980s, in their thirties and coming to positions of influence in organizations. The backwash of this movement may well have created a climate in which talk of empowerment and harmony had an appeal which at other times it might have lacked, for as Boltanski and Chiapello (2007) explain, the new managerialism took over much of the language of the 1960s' protest movement. And similar points could perhaps be made about the increasing acceptance of feminism and of women in organizations, which helped to foster a receptive atmosphere for what could be read by some as a move away from the macho management of more traditional approaches.

Regardless of the exact part played by these and other factors, my point is that the emergence and take-up of ideas about organizational culture happened within historical, economic and cultural contexts and was neither inevitable nor fortuitous. As I have repeatedly stressed, organization theory can never be separated from such contexts, and cannot be thought of as simply unfolding through some kind of natural or logical progression. Nor was it the case that the basic ideas of organizational culture had never been articulated before the 1980s – it is their widespread take-up which was lacking, presumably for lack of a context within which it made sense to do so. By the 1980s there existed, at least in the USA but also, with local twists, in the UK and elsewhere, that mixture of fear and hope that made a fertile soil for the embrace of culture management.

And embrace it they did. Culture was *the* word within organizations for the next two decades, and it continues to be part of the routine repertoire of managers and of organizational theorists to the present day. It's fair to say that some of the shine has gone off it – both through familiarity and because, as I will discuss in a minute, it has not really lived up to its promises – but the basic analysis of organizations that culture management contained remains at the heart of current managerial thinking, as we will see both in this chapter and the next one, notwithstanding the limitations of the techniques it proposes. Indeed, one index of those limitations is that of the 62 'excellent' companies profiled in Peters and Waterman's book, a large number had within a year ceased to meet the criteria of excellence and, within a few years, some had ceased to exist altogether. Perhaps that is not surprising in what the late Peter Drucker witheringly called the 'book for juveniles'; yet hundreds of similar books, typically extolling the virtues of one particular company at one particular time, were produced and sold in the following decades and form the basis of the endless case studies of 'best practice' used on management courses throughout the world. Hmm.

doing culture

Shallow as it undoubtedly was, the culture idea proposes more than that organizations should develop shared values. Rather, it identifies a whole range of organizational practices designed to elicit these values. And whilst the idea may have been shallow, the practices it promoted had as their aim, and sometimes their effect, something like the reconstitution of personhood. In Chapter 2 I talked about the ways in which human relations theory initiated a new domain for management in which people – or more accurately personhood – became a target for intervention and reshaping. In many respects culture management stands in this tradition, but I think that it entails a noticeable refinement and extension of it. Culture management is much more ambitious in its desire to shape people's beliefs than 'traditional' human relations. The latter tried, certainly, to 'adjust' employees to their workplace, but it also sought to design work around what were assumed to be a relatively stable and enduring set of human needs. The search for shared values entails a much more aggressive design agenda in which it is the worker, not the work, which is the main locus of management. Culture management aspires to intervene in and regulate being, so that there is no distance between individuals' purposes and those of the organization for which they work.

Some of the more obvious ways in which this is done include selection of staff who are, or appear to be, amenable to organizational values and, perhaps more controversially, the sacking of those existing employees who are not so amenable. Since culture management typically accompanies a 'downsizing' of managerial numbers, the opportunities for such sackings certainly exist. The application of culture management was very much at the heart of the changes brought by the large-scale privatizations of publicly owned organizations in the UK and elsewhere in the 1980s and 1990s. In addition to changing ownership, there was an agenda to shift the organizations from a public sector 'ethos' (or culture), which was presumed to be inefficient, towards a more business-like orientation. At the same time, there was an imperative to cut costs through redundancy. Thus many of those who were targeted for, or who took up offers of, redundancy were those who were unwilling or unable to 'commit' to the new culture. However, one difficulty of such an approach is that it may well (and in the case of the privatizations undoubtedly did) strip out those with the greatest degree of technical knowledge and experience of the services they offered.

But the adjustment of personnel according to who fits in is only the most superficial, and least novel, of the techniques which culture management brings to bear. More insidious is the use of all kinds of training, communication and what Peters and Waterman, with characteristic banality, called 'hoopla'. Employees are exposed to organizational values in the form of videos, mission statements, pocket-sized cards with core values printed upon them, company slogans, company songs, group exercises and a whole gamut of ever-more weird and wonderful happenings such as, in one UK bank, parades of employees in animal costumes chanting the virtues of the bank as a fun place to be!

This I think is pretty bizarre stuff, and perhaps of necessity it has to be. One interpretation of what is going on here is an attempt to produce Hawthorne effects of the sort discussed in Chapter 2. But these effects (as the Hawthorne Studies themselves showed) are short-lived. Therefore a search for novelty will always be needed to keep the momentum going. But, more importantly, most of the more extravagant examples of culture management need to operate at a symbolic level. Culture, after all, is not a tangible thing. We learn about cultures (whether societal or organizational) as it were indirectly – through the meaning which events appear to have. For example, the animal parade *symbolizes* the zany culture which it supposedly obtains. The manipulation of symbols provides some of the deepest techniques of culture management.

Company names and logos are an obvious example as these in some sense represent or symbolize the whole of the organization, both projecting it to the outer world of its markets and back into the organization in the form of its employees. It is no coincidence that the privatizations provide good examples of this. To take just one, the Yorkshire Electricity Board became Yorkshire Electricity after privatization. Why? Because 'board' sounds old-fashioned, bureaucratic, public sector-ish. But Yorkshire Electricity soon became YE, which sounds altogether more snazzy and less parochial. It also has the advantage of not really telling you what the company does, which is handy given that these organizations quickly diversified into non-traditional activities (handy, too, when the diversification embraces both electricity and water which don't in real, if not corporate, life mix too well). Such developments are also an aspect of the wider ways in which companies are increasingly detached from localities and communities, as discussed in detail in Chapter 5.

These shifting organizational identities clearly relate to attempts to shift employee identities[2], but of course they are relatively superficial.

More profound symbolic manipulations relate to things like architecture and clothing. One of the persistent ways in which shared values have been symbolized has been the erosion of many of the symbols of hierarchy in organizations like separate offices (instead of open plan), different floors of the building for different grades, differential access to parking, company cars and so on. In the motor industry, in particular, one idea imported from Japan in the 1980s was to have employees at all levels up to and including senior management wearing identical boiler suits, and all attending 'morning assemblies', which sometimes included the singing of company hymns. The symbolism of this was quite profound: it seemed to say that 'we' are all working for a common cause, each playing our own parts within it, but all parts equally valued, and the quasi-religious aspects are easy to see. The best-known example of this kind of culture management is that of Toyota, to the extent that 'Toyota-ism' is often used as a term, like Fordism, to sum up a generic way of organizing. Toyota culture is described uncritically, but in great detail, by Liker and Hoseus (2008) and it is no coincidence that the subtitle of this book refers to the 'heart and soul of the Toyota way', underscoring the incipient religiosity of the approach.

Then there are the hosts of rituals and stories designed to impact upon how people feel (an important word) about the organization. The supermarket boss whose childhood was spent selling cheap eggs from his satchel – symbolizing his lifelong commitment to good-value groceries. The Honda worker, referred to in Peters and Waterman, who on passing a Honda in the street will straighten its windscreen wipers because he cannot bear to see an imperfect Honda, symbolizing the commitment of Honda workers to quality (I find this story particularly creepy). The hotel receptionist who, on finding the hotel full, invites a desperate late-night arrival to stay in her spare room, symbolizing the commitment of the hotel chain's staff to its customers (that's pretty twee, as well). The New York advertising agency, described in a brilliant article by Michael Rosen (1988), which has a Christmas sketch show ritual in which senior managers are lampooned, symbolizing the democracy and informality of the firm. And the legions of organizations which have a 'dress-down Friday' to symbolize the unstuffy, egalitarian culture they purport to have (at least on Fridays).

The list goes on, and although each example in isolation perhaps doesn't mean much, their accumulation within an individual organization tends towards building – more or less convincingly – a story about the culture to which employees are invited to subscribe. But perhaps 'invited' is the wrong word (revealingly, attendance at the Christmas party Rosen describes was compulsory). First, because there are real sanctions on those who fail to do so – if you don't fit in, then you may well be first in line for the next set of redundancies. However, whilst true, that isn't really as important as the fact that, rather than being an 'invitation' to be accepted or refused, the most profound forms of culture management circumvent choice. In what is to my mind probably still the finest study of organizational culture management – Gideon Kunda's book *Engineering Culture* – one of the managers of the firm studied gives this chilling explanation: 'The idea is to educate people without them knowing it. Have the religion and not know how they got it' (Kunda, 1992: 5).

Again the invocation of the language of religion is significant as this underlines what has to be grasped in thinking about culture management. Its whole purpose is to reconstitute beliefs – nothing less will do if its promise of the removal of supervision is to be achieved. In its sophisticated manifestations, it uses techniques by no means dissimilar to those of religious cults. It demands of the employee a total commitment to the organization, and although in some of its early manifestations in 'Japanese' management this was sometimes matched by an organizational commitment to lifetime employment, nowadays it is demanded even as employment is more insecure and temporary. Indeed, even when you are considered for temporary, mundane jobs such as supermarket shelf-stacking, you are likely to be expected to display enthusiasm and excitement about corporate values. Such demands can be understood as eroding the barrier between the private, 'real' or 'free' self and the public realm of work, for to be truly committed, to 'have the religion' does not allow such a separation. As more recent studies than Kunda's have shown (e.g. Fleming and Spicer, 2004; Costas and Fleming, 2009) the aspiration of culture management is that the individual employee be not partially or superficially committed, but wholly and 'authentically' so.

what's wrong with all this?

I don't really know where to start. I suppose the most obvious question is to ask whether cultures really can be managed in this way. From the very early days of the culture frenzy there were voices saying that it could not. Linda Smircich (1983) was one of the first of these. She suggested that organizational culture could be thought of in at least two ways. In one version, culture was a 'critical variable', in another a 'root metaphor'. What she meant by the first term (I'll come back to the second later) was that culture management assumed that culture could indeed be managed – that it was amenable to intervention, control and definition, that it was a critical variable. This was clearly the assumption of those who advocated it. After all, to write about culture management but then admit that it wasn't actually manageable would be slightly odd. But it is plain that these advocates had much more in mind than the proposition that culture could be managed. Pascale and Athos (1982) had talked about shared values as one of the 'levers' of management and they clearly believed that culture could be treated as if it were part of an organizational machine in which controls were manipulated at the whim of managers.

So culture management says more than that culture can be controlled. It also proposes that it be controlled in particular directions. After all, shared values or strong culture don't say anything at all about what those values are, or what that strength consists of. For example, we might envisage an organization in which the employees had shared values that said that they should sit around drinking tea. But would this be the kind of organization anticipated by the culture management advocates? I think we can say that the answer is 'no'. More than that, we can say that *of course* the answer is 'no'. Culture management imagines a world in which shared values are directed towards the goal of productivity, whether as quantity or quality. So, suddenly, the freedom and empowerment envisaged by culture management takes on a new hue: these supposedly progressive goals are only on offer if the employees accept that their efforts must be directed towards the profitability of the company. One index of this is the way that, although in principle, a culture specifies what is *distinctive* about an organization, in practice the cultures sought by organizations involve a very limited and extremely repetitious set of pieties: customer service, quality, flexibility and innovation being the watchwords. Why? Because these are the attributes which senior managers believe will deliver competitive advantage.

And this is the thing about culture management. It is based upon the idea that cultural values are hierarchically defined – that is defined by senior managers or by head office. Linda Smircich's (1983) analysis says that there is a different way of viewing culture. Culture as root metaphor, as Smircich dubs it, says that, yes, organizations have cultures but these are spontaneous, unmanaged, just the way things are. It is a culture, certainly, but it doesn't necessarily conform to what managers want. Culture as root metaphor means something the organization *is* rather than something it *has*. People in organizations do things, they work together in a certain way: that's the culture. It is natural, spontaneous and, in short, it is what it is.

This is a nice dichotomy that has been influential in the literature and which captures something of the reality of organizations – two things that don't always go together, by the way. But where does it take us? For some analysts, of whom Meek (1988) is perhaps the most articulate, the answer is that since culture is just what it is, then it is relatively impervious to intervention. A good way of thinking about this is in terms of stories. Of course it is true that stories go round organizations and that these define something of the culture. But it doesn't follow that the stories manufactured and put around by culture managers gain much purchase. These are normally cringe-inducing stories about sycophantic employees giving great service. As such, they don't have much chance of being taken seriously when compared with more grounded stories about how, say, a manager never turns up for work and relies upon subordinates to cover for him (or her; no, let's say it's him).

So there is a 'real', spontaneous culture and a 'managed', imposed culture on top of this. And this means that attempts by managers to speak lightly of changing 'the culture' have to be treated as, at best, no more than optimism. There is plenty of evidence to back up this jaundiced analysis. In an interesting paper from early on in the application of culture management, Ogbonna and Wilkinson (1988) look at supermarket staff. The staff were encouraged to embrace a corporate culture of 'customer service', which entailed smiling at customers and being friendly so as to make them feel valued. The studies showed that the staff did not embrace the culture management programme, but did conform superficially to its demands. They 'smiled but did not mean it' and did so because they were aware that cameras and mystery shoppers were checking on them. Similar things have been found by later studies, such as that of a large Australian call centre promoting the kind of zany, fun ethos of the sort mentioned earlier (Fleming, 2005). Again, the idea was that this would promote a customer service ethos of friendliness and informality. Here employees were encouraged to see work as a form of play, supported by a multiplicity of rituals such as fancy dress days and so on, but it was experienced by many of the staff as an imposition which was 'cheesy' and condescending. Thus they pretended to be enjoying themselves whilst inwardly resenting and rejecting the 'fun' culture.

Now these are very revealing studies. You might think that if the staff are doing what is expected of them by 'the culture' then culture management has succeeded. But of course a moment's thought shows that this is not true. For culture management requires that staff 'really' believe in the values, not just that they go along with them in case a camera found that they were not smiling, or a manager spotted them not being zany enough. And it requires it not just for some theoretical reason but because unless staff really embrace the desired customer service culture then the costs of managing and monitoring them will not be saved.

Let me give a sharper example, again from supermarkets. I once had a part-time MBA student who was a senior manager in a supermarket chain which was known as an exemplar of successful culture management, and featured on management courses as a good practice case study in this area. This case study presented survey evidence to show the wide extent of buy-in to corporate culture values. My student wanted to test the extent to which front-line staff subscribed to these corporate values. The staff had just been subject to a multimillion-pound culture training initiative. My student found, not that staff did not believe in the values, but that three-quarters of them claimed never to have *heard* of the values.

This kind of example really needs to be taken seriously for two reasons. One, which is the most important for this chapter, is that attempts at culture management don't necessarily work. And perhaps they particularly don't work when the targets are low-paid workers in front-line positions. It makes little financial sense to devote huge resources to their cultural training – most are temporary and part-time workers – even though they are the ones who interact with customers. So the typical approach is to show them a video or two and hope for the best. The second thing we should take from this example is that many of those exciting case studies which management courses urge upon their students are, well, kind of crap. They reflect what managers say about organizations, not – or not necessarily – the lived experience of those who work in them.

So, if we are sensible, we will be sceptical about the more grandiose claims of culture management. Does this mean we can ignore them altogether? No, for attempts to manage culture *are* part of organizational culture and can't be discounted so lightly. Although that supermarket example suggests that culture management may have relatively little purchase, it doesn't follow that this is necessarily the case. Kunda's (1992) study of the engineering firm 'Tech' is a good example of this, because it shows how the values promoted by culture management do get taken up and used in everyday practice and language by the firm's employees. Kunda does show, however, that the way in which this happens is much more mixed and ambiguous than the proponents of culture management recognize.

For these reasons, it is important to tread a path which, whilst duly suspicious of the claims that culture can be unproblematically managed, avoids lapsing into 'cultural purism'. This is the term used by my former colleague Hugh Willmott in his landmark paper on organizational culture management (Willmott, 1993). He believes that culture management has to be taken seriously because of the potential it offers to reformulate identity and meaning in line with managerial *diktat*. His suggestion, and it is one made by several analysts of culture, is that it is a particular form of control which seeks to operate not by the external regulation of behaviour, but by shaping the internal world, the identity, of people at work. I share this view, and it is implicit in what I have already written. But Willmott goes rather further than this, in making a comparison between culture management and George Orwell's (1949) brilliant fictional description of a future totalitarian society in the novel *Nineteen Eighty-Four*.

I have perhaps already prefigured this by talking about the way that values are defined hierarchically in organizational culture, but there is more to it than that. In *Nineteen Eighty-Four*, Orwell draws upon his knowledge of the totalitarian regimes of Nazi Germany and the Stalinist Soviet Union (and, it seems, interestingly in this context, from his reading of Burnham's account of the managerial revolution – see Orwell, 1946) to point to certain features of such regimes. These include, famously, 'Big Brother', better known in the UK now as the name of a TV programme which observes a group of fairly awful people in the hope (often realized) that they will do something gross. Orwell's Big Brother is the patriarchal dictator who constantly monitors members of society for incorrect behaviour (it is this theme of surveillance, of course, which links the Orwell novel with the TV show). This behaviour is not confined to overt subversion but to departures from orthodoxy of any sort. Part and parcel of this is a language, 'Newspeak', which by refining the range of what can be expressed places ever-more restricted limits around what can be thought. The society is characterized by monstrous, counter-intuitive slogans, such as 'freedom is slavery', the invocation of enemy hordes which will destroy the society and an emphasis, for members of the Party, on communal activities and the abnegation of the individual in favour of the collective good.

I think – and here I am going further than Willmott, and probably being less subtle – that there are many parallels to be drawn between Orwell's nightmare vision of the future and culture management. In culture management, there is very often the construction of a heroic leader (it is noteworthy that many culture management stories concern such leaders) and there is intensive use of surveillance methods. One of the richest veins of organization theory in recent years has been the use of the 'post-structuralist' ideas of Michel Foucault (1979) to explore surveillance at work. Foucault famously analysed the panoptic prison in which prisoners could be watched but would not know when they were being watched. Over time, such a situation would lead to the prisoners becoming self-disciplining. I will come back to this in a moment, but just to continue the parallels with *Nineteen Eighty-Four*, culture management is very much concerned with promoting corporate languages and slogans, and typically encourages employees to believe that 'the competition' will destroy the organization if they are not compliant to managerial demands.

More than anything – and this is more Hugh Willmott's point – totalitarianism, as in *Nineteen Eighty-Four*, invokes the collectivity and elevates this above the individual. The individual both matters less than the collective but, also, finds him or herself through alignment with and subservience to the collective. This was certainly a feature of both Nazi and Stalinist regimes, as well as of other cases of totalitarian society. Culture management, in a similar way, impinges on autonomy but, in an insidious twist, claims that it actually promotes autonomy ('freedom is slavery' to use one of the infamous slogans of Orwell's novel). This is the nexus of issues around empowerment. As I suggested earlier, empowerment in organizations has the curious feature that it is only allowed if it is exercised in ways beneficial to the organization. Willmott makes the more general point that empowerment cannot meaningfully be *bestowed* upon others but can only be meaningful if it is *achieved* by people themselves.

How seriously should we take all this? I'm not quite sure. There are some fairly obvious limitations to the analogy with *Nineteen Eighty-Four*. In the novel, the central character, Winston Smith, is taken to a torture chamber, subjected to grotesque violence and has his character reprogrammed through sophisticated psychological techniques. Someone who resists an organizational culture is not going to be treated this way. At worst, they will be sacked. Relatedly, people can choose whether they work for an organization which manages its culture; people in totalitarian societies typically cannot. But this isn't quite the end of the story. People in our society do suffer economically and in other ways if they do not work, and most large companies do use some form of culture management (still, people could work for a small company, or be self-employed). And we can certainly imagine some people – perhaps those who are relatively old, with poor chances of being employed elsewhere and with a family to support – enduring a certain amount of humiliation and bullying rather than lose their job. Even so, it is important, not least because of the need not to blunt our wariness of full-blown totalitarianism, to see that this is an imperfect analogy, even if it captures a certain reality.

surveillance, choice and self-management

I want to talk about this a little more by returning to the issue of surveillance. There is much more to Foucault's work than the panoptic prison, and much more that is of great significance for organization theory (particularly good explanations of this are Knights, 1992 and Burrell, 1988). This leads some of those who are interested in Foucault to be rather 'sniffy' about the way that so much attention has been given to 'panopticism'. But I disagree. Surveillance is an important part of people's organizational experience – and was recognized as such long before Foucault's work – and the panopticon is a very illuminating way of exploring it. There are many examples. In wider society, examples include CCTV cameras, marketing databases, mobile phone tracking and DNA databases. In the workplace, it is becoming increasingly common to track employees' movements through smart cards. The supermarket 'mystery shopper' mentioned earlier is another case. The way that call centre operators have their calls monitored to check that they are using the right words, and dealing with the call at maximum speed is another, as is the measurement of call throughput.

Of course there are plenty of other examples of surveillance too, but the last of those just given are relevant for two reasons. One is that they are linked, specifically, to culture (for example, and especially, cultures promoting the value of customer service). The other is that they are cases not just of surveillance but of panoptic surveillance, in the sense that people don't know whether or not they are being observed at any particular time – so-called discontinuous surveillance. This is important as it is this which leads to the proposition of self-management through the internalization of norms of working. Other forms of surveillance – the entire genre of activities called 'overseeing' – do not necessarily have this quality in that they are continuous rather than discontinuous. This means that they work, if they do work, on the basis of compliance with external regulation, and the assumption is that if the overseeing ceases, then so too does the compliance. This is certainly a form of control but it is not one which can be used to support the claim that culture management represents an insidious reshaping of the self. What is perhaps surprising at first glance is that continuous surveillance, for all that it may be considered irksome, is actually less disciplinary in Foucauldian terms than discontinuous surveillance, in that the former remains external monitoring whereas the latter becomes, potentially, internalized.

One of the most widely quoted studies in this vein is Sewell and Wilkinson's (1992) paper on surveillance in an electronics factory. They argue that new manufacturing techniques, especially those involving total quality management (TQM) and just-in-time management (JIT), which are linked to the promotion of a culture of quality, offer particularly intense forms of surveillance, both electronically and through the peer pressure imposed by teams, leading to the self-imposition of high output levels. Sewell and Wilkinson spend a lot of time explaining the ways in which the workplace is like a panoptic prison. Actually the original design for the prison, by Jeremy Bentham, was inspired by the workshop run by Bentham's brother. The model therefore derives from the workplace in the first instance.

But that is a detail. The key question is whether, either in the prison or in the workplace, surveillance does in fact lead to self-regulating behaviour. Sewell and Wilkinson have been criticized for presenting too deterministic a picture of surveillance, as if its existence has a necessary effect in terms of self-regulation. On the one hand, it may be that people do not in fact work as hard as they can, but find all kinds of ways of getting round surveillance systems. On the other hand, even if they do work as hard as they can, it does not follow that this is because they have internalized disciplines, just that they are scared of getting caught out. By extension, this whole genre of work has been criticized for a lack of attention to the ways in which people in organizations resist or subvert control, somewhat ironically given the fact that resistance was one of Foucault's major preoccupations.

This clearly relates back to the earlier issue about the extent to which culture management can be thought of as analogous to totalitarianism and corrosive of autonomy and choice. The totalitarian analogy would suppose that resistance would be very limited (although, as the observed realities of totalitarian regimes suggest, never entirely absent). At a more theoretical level this is illuminated by an exchange between the sociologist Anthony Giddens, who tends to be sceptical of Foucauldian claims, and the organization theorist Gibson Burrell, who was one of those who first applied post-structuralist analysis to the study of organizations. Giddens (1984) argues that Foucault's work rests on the over-extension of what applies in 'total institutions' (for example, prisons, poorhouses, the army) to organizations in general. This ignores the rather specific features of total institutions, the most obvious being that you cannot normally leave them, and spend your entire life inside them. This is likely to mean that the kinds of subjects or identities produced within them will be of a rather unusual kind. Burrell's (1988) counter to this argument is summed up by the interesting observation that whilst we may not spend our lives in total organizations, the organization of our lives is total. In other words, that there is no escape from living in an organized way and this inevitably impinges upon our subjectivity. This is a more deterministic argument, in that it suggests little opportunity for choice and no possibility of meaningful escape.

In line with my general aim of accessibility I have not done anything like justice to the complexities of this debate, but I hope that I have given enough indication of its main contours. It is not, of course, possible to make a final pronouncement on what is the right answer. But my feeling, for what little it is worth, is that what is at issue here is a need to think in a much more subtle way about what is entailed in choice than is normal, either in organization theory or elsewhere. Consider the objection to thinking of culture management as totalitarian being that people can choose to leave the organization if they wish. The point, though, is not that culture management is totalitarian because it holds on to people who want to leave (and in this regard, it *is* different to totalitarian states); it is that it exerts a hold over people such that they do not wish to do so. The evidence for totalitarianism, therefore, is not confounded by the existence of choice but by the way in which that choice is used.

Developing from Foucault's work, both on subjectivity in general and on governmentality in particular (Foucault, 1991), Nikolas Rose has presented an analysis of the way that self-governing subjects emerge as 'entrepreneurs of themselves, shaping their own lives through the choices they make among the forms of life open to them' (Rose, 1989: 226) so that 'the Citizen, in work as much as outside it, is engaged in a project to shape his or her life as an autonomous individual driven by motives of self-fulfilment' (1989: 115). However, the contemporary preoccupation with choice has a distinct irony for, as Strathern (1992) points out, in such cultures we have no choice but to make choices. Not only this, but the consequences of our choices will be our own responsibility. You've had a heart attack? You shouldn't have chosen to eat so much fatty food. Not enough pension? You should have chosen to save more. Failed your exams? You should have chosen to work harder. In these senses, choice is to be understood not in terms of the expression of freedom, but as a disciplining and 'responsibilizing' process whose power is obscured, or, rather, magnified by the sense it gives of freedom (see Schwartz, 2004 for a very clear explanation of this apparent paradox). Choice is therefore not an alternative to control, but, rather, the way in which we exercise choice is expressive of control, including, most especially, those things which we do not experience as choice but understand to be 'just the way things are'.

From this perspective, the issue of the panopticon and surveillance also looks rather different. I don't at all want to decry the attention which has been paid to organizational surveillance mechanisms, which are real, important and often oppressive. However, they tend to think about the panopticon in rather literal ways – as physical (even if, often, 'virtual') artefacts. I think that a more important implication comes if we think about the panopticon metaphorically. The surveillance studies *do* use the panopticon metaphorically when they say something along the lines of 'the call centre is *like* the panoptic prison', but they treat it as if it were a discrete 'thing' rather than a kind of nebulous idea. It then becomes something contestable, resistible or embraceable. But what seems more profound to me are those parts of our 'taken for granted' which disappear from sight as things to be contested, resisted or embraced. These constitute the important stuff; because then the choices happen by default.

Imagine a group of students sitting in the lecture hall, taking notes. Of course they have a choice; they could leave, they could not take notes. And of course they are subject to disciplines (registers, tests) which would tend to prevent them doing so. Sometimes they don't turn up; sometimes they don't take notes – their behaviour isn't determined by the existence of those disciplines and they sometimes resist them. But they could also burst into song or remove all their clothes. And this they never do (or not in my experience, anyway). They don't need to *think* not to do so, and thus although they are making a choice they do not experience it as such. It is these taken-for-granted choices which form part of the fabric of our being which seem to me to be expressive of the more profound forms of self-discipline, and it presumably derives from strongly embedded socialization processes which exist (although of course in different forms and with different outcomes) in all societies. These deep and diffuse socialization processes are the important sense, I think, in which our lives are totally in organizations and in which panoptic metaphors have their most important purchase.

In terms of the workplace, people's behaviour is clearly proscribed in the same way as it is in the lecture theatre – there are a range of basic, obvious behaviours which we discipline ourselves about. Their obviousness makes them boring, perhaps even invisible, but from my point of view it is what makes them interesting and important. Many of these disciplines are quite general, nothing to do with the workplace at all. Others are more specific – our acceptance that we should turn up more or less on time and do more or less what we are told (and, sure, some people manage neither of these things). Both general and specific cases are an outcome of socialization, and also no doubt an ongoing medium of socialization (in the sense that our adherence to prescribed behaviours is reinforced by the constant observation of how others behave).

So, then, what about culture management? The point, I think, is that this too attempts a socialization process with a view to prescribing and proscribing behaviour through the adoption of certain values. Culture management proposes a version of 'the way things are' and invites us to take it as so. Indeed, it is surely no coincidence that one of the most commonly used and easily remembered definitions of organizational culture – so ubiquitous that it is attributed to all kinds of authors – is 'the way we do things around here'.

For this reason, culture management deserves to be criticized because it is indeed an attempt to gain an insidious form of control. It may be that socialization processes are in some sense necessary in any society;

it doesn't follow that these processes should be aimed at binding the individual into the attempt to gain competitive advantage for the organizations they work for. For sure, what culture management does in this regard is sometimes clumsy and ineffective. But I don't think we should judge it less harshly just because it isn't very good at its job or is attempted on the cheap. If it is an attempt to exert insidious control, is it any better if it fails to do so?

Anyway, if we're looking at an insidious control of what is defined as normal or natural, maybe culture management isn't so ineffective. I've mentioned some of the studies which show that culture management can regulate identity and the way people treat some things as natural and normal. It's very likely the case that those most liable to be affected in this way are not the rank and file employees like supermarket workers and call centre operatives, but more senior people – the managers and professionals in organizations. This is an interesting idea, because it suggests that what is at stake in culture management is not a kind of managerial domination of the working classes. Let me try to explain. Much conventional organization theory sees the workforce as in need of control, direction and co-ordination, and devises various ways of achieving this, of which culture management may be one such. It is assumed that managers themselves are already committed to organizational goals and values – at a basic level, that they will work hard and act responsibly. This conventional view has an ironic counterpart amongst some more radical commentators, who see the working classes as subject to the power of managers acting in ways perfectly in tune with the profit-seeking motives of their shareholders (Braverman, 1974).

Yet, as I suggested in Chapter 2, management had to be 'made' responsible, and at many periods in time this could not be assumed. What now appears quite normal and natural is that managers will work long hours, do whatever needs to be done to get the job done and are motivated to do so by the intrinsic interest of their work, the payment they receive and, in general, a sense of responsibility and professionalism. That same professionalism, unsurprisingly, informs the conduct of, precisely, professionals like doctors, lawyers and accountants – even academics. We don't think of these people as being 'empowered to delight the customer' or enrolled in 'joy gangs' (to use one of the ugliest pieces of culture-speak). Yet it is they who have most obviously taken to heart a set of norms about values and behaviour, learned, certainly, through general education, but also through the organizational processes of their workplaces, professional associations and so on. Of course this doesn't mean that such people never betray trust, are never lazy or even corrupt. But, to a very large extent, they exhibit a great deal of the self-management associated with culture management, and the occasions where they do not do so are remarkable as a result.

As I write these words it is a Sunday afternoon, and I have been working all weekend. I am on sabbatical in France and there is absolutely no one who knows or cares whether I am working or not. On some of my work I have imposed deadlines to meet, but for this book the deadlines are hazy and some way off. But I am still working, rather than doing any of the other things I could do with my weekend. Why? The obvious answer is because I choose to do so. That's true – but that is the whole point of the earlier discussion I gave about choice. It's the way I exercise choice which makes me self-managed, and that self-management is both part of my own identity and a part of the occupational and organizational cultures of academics.

This is not necessarily a 'bad thing'. It gets books written (well, that may not be such great news), it keeps organizations going, it delivers medical care in a responsible way and so on. But that isn't really the point. After all, the loyalty of party members in totalitarian regimes keeps the system going and is often associated with spectacular feats of industrial progress and military conquest which, at least for members of such societies, may be seen as no 'bad thing'. So the point is, more, to see how culture does exert a power – a power to produce values and behaviour.

In any case, 'not necessarily' are big words. The cultural production of self-management is, I would suggest, something present in and perhaps necessary to all social relations, although for sure the form it will take varies. The key issue is the way that this culture is developed and the uses to which it is put. I suppose this is another version of the question of instrumental and substantive rationality, discussed in Chapter 1. Cultures which develop through time, negotiation and which are put to uses that have some kind of dignity and substantive value are one thing, and perhaps some of the professions are examples of this. But culture management in modern organizations typically has few of these characteristics. It develops not through time and negotiation but as a 'programme' devised by a small number of people and projected onto other people either as an imposition or (more effectively) through guile. Moreover, it proposes a use which seems to lack dignity and value. It invokes the bastardized language of a counter-culture animated by a desire for individual freedom in the service of organizational conformity. To invite or seduce people to devote their whole being to producing cars, hamburgers or insurance policies seems to me a substantial negation of the possibilities that human existence might otherwise have. That these tawdry schemes often fail to secure their aims is a testimony to the good sense of those exposed to them, but in no way negates the presumption and arrogance of those devising them.

███████ conclusion

In this chapter I have tried to think through one of the central issues in contemporary organization. What I mean to imply by calling it that is the idea that 'culture' is not simply a specific topic within organization theory but is more like the *leitmotif* of a whole assembly of recent ways in which organizations have developed. Take any example – total quality management (TQM), business process re-engineering (BPR or just process re-engineering), the learning organization, Six Sigma (effectively TQM by a different name), the lean organization (or just 'lean') or the generic case of 'post-bureaucracy' discussed in the next chapter – and you will find an appeal to the need to create an appropriate organizational culture. Moreover, culture, like all these other examples, is crucially concerned with the promotion of self-managing, self-disciplined individuals. This centrality of culture management to organizations over recent decades is important to recall, especially when the term itself is not used. Partly because of its now long history of problems and contradictions, it is the case that many organizations avoid referring explicitly to culture management because it seems tainted. Yet the underlying ideas and practices continue to be present. Equally, the accumulated experience of culture management is likely to mean that those exposed to it are more aware of and reflective about its contradictions (perhaps in part as more and more people study courses which explain these). For example, recent studies have suggested that those expected to be 'authentic' at work experience a kind of knowingness about the ways in which this authenticity is also fake and alien (Costas and Fleming, 2009). So the way that culture management is attempted and experienced may change over time but the underlying theme of attempting to create and shape values and beliefs in the workplace remains a key aspect of contemporary organizational life.

Culture management represents both an obvious continuation of, but also something of a break with, the classical approaches to organization theory. It is a continuation in that it picks up on and develops the human relations concerned with personhood as a focus for managerial attention and as an organizational resource. Moreover, as this implies, it exemplifies the themes identified in the previous chapters of a preoccupation with instrumental rationality and control. It is a break in the scale of its ambitions with respect to self-management. It would certainly be wrong to ignore that self-management was an aim of many older approaches, again most obviously human relations theory. However, even the latter remained connected to a wider project for 'external' management since, as I suggested in Chapter 2, it was at least in part related to the promotion of a managerial elite with expertise in human relations. For sure the contemporary approaches create expert elites – consultants and managers with know-how in culture – but they also run alongside the erosion of the large cadre of middle managers, discussed in Chapter 5. Thus, the focus on the 'internal management' of the individual is all the more relentless, for culture management promotes *management* just as it demotes *managers*.

But for all that culture has been central to recent organizational theory and practice, it is only one part of a matrix of wider developments. These purport to represent a fundamental change in which the basic template of bureaucratic organization is in the process of being displaced by a new form – post-bureaucracy – which is required by the supposedly unprecedented changes of the contemporary world. In the next chapter I will explore this brave new world.

notes

1 Needless to say, this was a wildly optimistic picture of the Japanese economy in the 1970s and 1980s. It depicted, at the very best, life in the big corporations. That life was much harder than might be imagined, but for sure it was nothing when compared with the Japanese economy in general. During the Japanese 'economic miracle' probably three-quarters of the economy was not in the big companies but in its subcontractors who used migrant labour in camps where conditions were extraordinarily harsh. See Kamata (1982) for a horrifying account of the realities of what made the Japanese economy competitive. Current 'competitive pressures' derive from, and are used to justify, unregulated 'export processing zones' in the Developing World where beatings, torture of trade unionists and sub-subsistence wages are the norm (see Klein, 2000), and progressively degraded conditions for the working class in the Developed World (see Perelman, 2005).

2 The concept of identity is obviously an important one for understanding organizational culture but for reasons of space I just refer to it in passing and without detailed analysis. See Kenny, Whittle and Willmott (2011) for an up-to-date and comprehensive discussion.

4

Post-Bureaucracy and Change Management

The future is made of the same stuff as the present.

Simone Weil

With the exception of smoking and paedophilia there is probably nothing which these days attracts such hostility as bureaucracy. Certainly if you open just about any book on management and organizations, you will find, in some form or other, a very similar argument. It says that a bureaucratic way of organizing, whilst perhaps of some value in the dim and distant past, is completely unsuited to today's rapidly changing world and either has been, or must now be, swept away in favour of a range of new organizational forms. These are given many different names – the post-Fordist, networked or even postmodern organization – but as an umbrella term we can call them 'post-bureaucracies'. Charles Heckscher (1994) goes so far as to assert that it is possible to identify a post-bureaucratic ideal-type, in contrast to Weber's ideal-type of bureaucracy. In outline, it consists of the following characteristics:

- Rules are replaced with consensus and dialogue based upon personal influence rather than status. People are trusted to act on the basis of shared values rather than rules.
- Responsibilities are assigned on the basis of competence for tasks rather than hierarchy, and are treated as individuals rather than impersonally.
- The organization has an open boundary, so that rather than full-time permanent employment, people come into and out of the organization in a flexible way including part-time, temporary and consultancy arrangements. Work is no longer done in fixed hours or at a designated place.

It's easy to pick out two things from this description. One is that it does indeed run counter to the precepts of bureaucracy, although like much that is contemporary in organization theory, it grows out of the classical approaches, in this case of human relations theory. Rules, hierarchy, career structures, impersonality are all swept away. The other is that this represents both a re-articulation of, and a departure from, the ideas about culture management. A re-articulation because of its stress on shared values. And a departure because it envisages not a fixed collective of organizationally socialized and disciplined (or 'empowered') employees but a floating complement of staff only intermittently and perhaps fleetingly associated with the organization. So it takes over all of the problems of the culture model but it also adds some new ones. For if it is questionable whether an organization can inculcate 'shared values' in its permanent workforce, then how much more questionable must it be for such values to obtain within such transitory attachments?

There are several ways in which we can and should mock and deride this kind of thinking. One, which I will come back to later in this chapter, is the cod history and sociology which informs this kind of 'new era' thinking. The way that Heckscher positions his 'ideal-type' as being on all fours with Weber's analysis of bureaucracy – founded as it was on massive and sustained scholarship – is actually the least objectionable. Heckscher is at least a serious and committed researcher, and, compared with most of those who trot out this kind of line, a sophisticated and insightful reasoner. But consider the work of Hammer and Champy (1993) who so influentially propounded the 'business process re-engineering revolution'. This too represents itself as an anti-bureaucratic creed (although, as even its name implies, it retains the imprint of the engineering approach of the most traditional versions of management). But unlike Heckscher, only the flimsiest of research is invoked to sustain the grandiloquent claim that re-engineering is comparable in scope and profundity with Adam Smith's discovery [sic] of the division of labour (Hammer and Champy, 1993: 5). This is the kind of 'epochal' claim which du Gay (2003) identifies as typical of critiques of bureaucracy.

A second way of pricking the presumption of the post-bureaucratic case is one which carefully documents just how flimsy its reality claims are. Paul Thompson and his collaborators, through a series of detailed studies of both aggregate statistical evidence and individual cases, have shown that job structures and work experiences have been remarkably unaltered by the post-bureaucratic revolution. They suggest that its claims have conflated several different trends so that whereas the rise of the service economy is an undoubted trend in advanced industrial societies, what it typically means is the growth of low-skilled and standardized jobs in, for example, catering, telesales and call centres (Warhurst and Thompson, 1998). From a similar kind of perspective, Rick Delbridge's work – which is one of the best of more recent contributions to a distinguished tradition of workplace ethnographies – has called into question the extent of post-bureaucratic transformation (Delbridge, 1998).

The study reports on Delbridge's time in two British factories. One is a Japanese-owned electronics plant (Nippon CTV), the other a European-owned producer of automotive components (ValleyCo). Although strictly speaking this is not a study of bureaucracy and post-bureaucracy, it does contrast the more traditional approach at ValleyCo with the 'japanized' approach at Nippon CTV where there is a focus on lean production, just-in-time management, innovation, customer focus and HRM – all the paraphernalia of the post-bureaucratic workplace.

Whilst Delbridge found a number of contrasts between the plants, it is fair to say that his overall conclusion is that there is a considerable similarity between 'traditional' and 'new' forms of working in terms of things like hierarchy, participation or trust:

> There is little to suggest that contemporary manufacturing is best characterised as 'postfordist' and that the shop-floor is a hotbed of worker autonomy and knowledge creation. (Delbridge, 1998: 192)

These kinds of studies might seem like the best way of countering the claims of post-bureaucracy's flagwavers. They certainly act as an antidote to the extravagant and self-serving claims such as those contained within Ricardo Semler's (1993) account of his firm Semco, a Brazilian engineering firm. Semler regards himself as a 'counsellor' rather than a chief executive, and this illustrates the idea that post-bureaucracy discounts hierarchy. Overall, Semco is characterized by an approach which rejects formal rules, where employees set their own working hours and pay rates, and which is relaxed about unionization and strike activity. But this account downplays the way that the 'new' Semco was predicated upon wholesale redundancies in the old corporation. These are mentioned, but as necessary blows against bureaucratic inertia and without any attention to what the experiences of the downsized bureaucrats might be (did they starve to death? We don't know and, in Semler's narrative, are given no reason to care). More importantly, unlike studies such as that of Delbridge, we hear nothing at all of the voice and experience of those who actually work there. We are simply invited to take on trust the organization as refracted through Semler's lens.

Is, say, Thompson right? Is Semler wrong? These are endlessly contestable questions. The adequacy of evidence selected and the adequacy of the way it is interpreted are crucial; but this adequacy will be assessed in the light of pre-existing prejudices, arguments and views. So, for all their virtues, I wonder if empirical refutations of the post-bureaucracy thesis are enough. They help, of course, but they rest on a perhaps naïve assumption that the facts will, or can, speak for themselves. Unfortunately, that does not really meet the cunning of the opposition. They will respond that the kinds of developments discussed by the critics are 'not really' post-bureaucracy and that, in any case, whilst instances of post-bureaucracy may be thin on the ground they are, nonetheless, the future of organizations. They will find particular examples that conform to the case, and these examples may be well-founded. If pushed, they may even say that for all that the world is not so very post-bureaucratic, it would be better if it were. Indeed it is striking that the 'war on bureaucracy' rather like those on drugs or terrorism seems never to be won. Somehow, bureaucracy is about to disappear yet somehow, decade after decade, it remains an omnipresent enemy to be defeated.

So what is needed (alongside empirical counter-examples) is a way of questioning the very structure, presumptions and assumptions of the post-bureaucratic argument. Shift the terms of debate and you shift the filter through which any evidence is evaluated. Apart from mocking its presumptuousness and questioning its evidence, a third way of doing this is to question the desirability of the post-bureaucratic model as an ideal – whether or not it exists. An example is Paul du Gay's (2000) argument about bureaucracy, mentioned in Chapter 1. Here, the case was made that bureaucracy, for all its critics, embodies an ethic of fairness which is bound up with impersonal treatment. Critics may complain that it dehumanizes, but they miss the protection this offers.

Heckscher's post-bureaucracy points up very sharply what is at stake here. Post-bureaucracy does away with the turgid old nonsense about impersonality, yearly promotions and fixed salary scales in favour of individual treatment where reward is based on merit. How refreshing; for which of us wishes to be treated as anything other than an individual? Which of us wishes to get the same pay rise, after all the work we have done, as the time-serving hack at the next desk? Fine. So, now, how is our pay rise going to be determined? By performance? But who will judge this performance? Perhaps – as with the case for and against post-bureaucracy – the facts will speak for themselves. The difficulty is that there is an endless range of contextual factors to individual performance that any assessor may (and very likely will) be unable to determine. Personal treatment means treatment at whim. It may be overtly corrupt – those with pretty faces get the best deal. It may just depend upon the sincerely held judgements of our assessors. Either way, our desire to be treated individually can conflict sharply with our desire to be treated fairly. And suddenly, post-bureaucracy recedes as a utopian ideal and comes into focus as potentially a site of prejudice and incompetence.

why are you always carping?

If you have followed the argument so far but are not persuaded by it, then you may well be thinking something along these lines: will nothing ever satisfy you? Older approaches to organizations have been condemned as dehumanizing and degrading. Human relations-type approaches are manipulative. Culture management is brainwashing. Now we have non-hierarchical, personally focused and trust-based organizations and you are still whinging. Your sort make me sick. Well, let's see.

The problem is that the rhetoric of post-bureaucracy is considerably more appealing than its consequences. These are most obvious in relation to public sector organizations, for it is these which capture political and public attention. To take some UK examples, in health there is a constant complaint about the bureaucratic targets set by meddling civil servants. Let individual hospitals determine what is best without the dead hand of bureaucracy. But when they do, inevitably differences arise between different areas. This is then depicted as the scandal of the 'postcode lottery', to which the solution can only be – centrally determined bureaucratic targets. Indeed, even as introducing more *localism* was being touted as a vital reform to NHS bureaucracy in order to achieve 'value for money', it was being reported as scandalous that lack of *centralized* purchase of supplies was leading to £1 billion per annum of waste (Smyth, 2011). Or in schools, where the accusation in the 1980s was that these were adopting all manner of dogmas, with sex education undermining responsible family life; history being taught in terms of capitalist and colonialist repression; even sport being denuded of the competitive ethic. The solution was to introduce centralized, bureaucratic methods of quality assurance and the prescription of a national curriculum. Roll forward to today and the complaint is that we have a restrictive, bureaucratic and centralized administration and the solution is to devolve power to school level. It doesn't take a genius to predict that as this solution is implemented then, in a few years time, there will be calls for centralized control to prevent the 'abuses' of local freedom. And we can expect this to happen across the UK public sector as the current government implements the ideas of 'chaos theory' in order to dismantle centralized bureaucracies and create 'big bang localism', as one of that government's key thinkers puts it (Boles, 2010).

At its most generic, the issue is that if systemic rules treat individuals badly then the call is for more discrimination for individuals, but if individual treatment results in bad outcomes then the call is for more rule-based systems. And it's not just in relation to public services that we put some premium on systemic, rule-based treatment. For example, most of us would expect an insurance company to treat like cases alike – in other words to enact bureaucratic standardization. This dilemma serves to point up some important issues (including how politics can deal with so contradictory a set of demands). One is that the design of organizations, whether in the public sector or not, is not some neutral, 'technical' issue in the way that managerial approaches to organization fantasize is the case. Assuming that – as is usually the case – the outputs of organizations matter to people, the way that they are organized must be the subject of different views and interests and therefore is necessarily in the domain of values and not just techniques. Second, these examples show that those who confidently propound a post-bureaucratic future display an ignorance about the very reasons why bureaucratic organizations emerged.

This is not to say that bureaucratic organizations are particularly praiseworthy. In Chapter 1, I outlined the various kinds of 'bureaucratic dysfunctionalism' that are part of what constitutes the case against bureaucracy. But there is also a post-bureaucratic dysfunctionalism, in which fairness, consistency and transparency are absent, which should be considered alongside any advantages the 'new model' may have. Perhaps more than anything else, bureaucracy with its procedures and its stifling routine, is said to prevent innovation, risk-taking and entrepreneurial zeal. This may be true, but it also protects us from the risks of ill-considered innovation and if it should come to be that the future is post-bureaucratic, it may well also be a future where spectacular failures occur; and if it is true that the outputs of organizations matter to people, then they may come to rue the day when risk was embraced with such recklessness. Indeed, in the wake of the financial crisis discussed in the next chapter, the way in which investment banks became so innovative with respect to developing new financial instruments, so cavalier about risk and so spectacularly failed as a result, might lead us to think that that day has already arrived.

A particular aspect of the case for post-bureaucracy as against the constraints of rule-based 'red tape' is that they are more 'agile' and can act much more quickly. A clear illustration of this can be found in the following example:

> The millionaire businessman Roy Aldridge ... boasts that his company Capita takes seven hours to make a decision reached in seven weeks by the civil service. (Chrisafis, 2003: 13)

But is speed necessarily good? Although Capita is a hugely successful company with a turnover in 2010 of almost £3 billion (albeit no longer headed by Rod Aldridge, who resigned in 2006 following unproven allegations that government contracts were linked to his donations to the Labour Party), it has been involved in a series of controversies (Chrisafis, 2003). Capita is one of the companies of choice for the UK government for the privatization and/or subcontracting of what had hitherto been state-provided services – from driving tests to defence contracts to the leasing of ambulances. The long list includes individual learning accounts (which collapsed amidst fraud); criminal records (which failed to vet teachers in time to allow the school year to commence on time); and housing benefits and television licences (both systems encountering serious problems). For this reason, the firm is referred to by the satirical magazine *Private Eye* as 'Crapita' (see Whitfield, 2011 for further information on some of Capita's recent activities).

The case of individual learning accounts, to take just one of these examples, is revealing. Launched in 2000, the scheme cost £268 million until its collapse in 2002 due to widespread fraud on the part of bogus training providers. The National Audit Office (NAO) investigated what had happened and its head, Sir John Bourn, said:

> ... the *speed* with which the Department [for Education and Skills] implemented the scheme resulted in corners being cut ... which made fraudulent activities possible. (NAO, 2002; *emphasis added*)

So the claim that post-bureaucracies are more efficient by virtue of being faster than bureaucracies does not get round the question which I raised in Chapter 1 with respect to bureaucracy: efficient in what respects and for whom?

But post-bureaucracy does not just entail claims about efficiency. It also claims a moral case of which the strongest aspect is that it addresses the dehumanization associated with bureaucracy. This is not a new claim, since it was also made for human relations approaches within traditional organizations. And as with those claims it founders on the grounds which I guess I have rehearsed ad nauseam already. Bureaucracy does dehumanize to the extent that it reduces its employees (and customers) to the level of cogs in the organizational machine. But the humanization envisaged by post-bureaucracy, like that found in culture management, offers only a truncated version of humanity – the freedom to align oneself with the organizational machine or be punished. The fact that the former tries to suppress human agency whilst the latter tries to harness it is scarcely a compelling difference. And the fact that the post-bureaucratic variant of culture management is to try to harness human agency without even offering stable employment in return makes it all the less appealing.

A moment ago, I referred to post-bureaucracy as a 'new model'. Why the speechmarks? Because all this talk of a new era and new organizational forms conceals or forgets the way that such claims are recurring so that it is possible to find, throughout organization theory, almost identical models of the future. To understand this amnesia, it is necessary to address what is probably the central aspect of contemporary approaches to studying organizations. If the most fundamental part of the classical approaches was the modernist assumption of manageability, its counterpart in contemporary approaches is the 'postmodernist' preoccupation with 'change'. Or, more accurately, the way that these two fundamentals are combined in the *sine qua non* of contemporary approaches – change management.

this changing world

What ties together almost all of the issues about culture management, post-bureaucracy and the contemporary preoccupations of mainstream organization theory is, I think, the centrality placed upon the concept of change. Change provides a kind of 'meta-narrative', an overarching rationale or assumption which then acts as an explicit or implicit justification for specific change programmes in organizations. So ubiquitous is the invocation of change, and so crucial is it to the claims which follow from it, that it seems reasonable to describe it as a fetish. Grint (1997: 35) refers to the fetish for change in an analysis of management fashions and fads, but its significance goes beyond these. Change is a notion which is drawn upon in a largely unthinking, but very significant, way so that it takes on an almost magical character. Change is like a totem before which we must prostrate ourselves and in the face of which we are powerless.

Perhaps the most interesting feature of the change fetish is the way in which it figures as the contextual, introductory and taken for granted. So obvious is it taken to be that it typically takes the form of rushed assertions at the outset of any particular treatment of organizations and management. For example, in one leading textbook:

> In a changing world the only constant is change … the reality is that the stability which seemed to characterise the corporate world in the 1950s and 1960s has given way to increased and global competition, technological innovation and change, limited resources, deregulation, privatisation of public sector organisations and change in much more besides. (Carnall, 1995: 1)

This quotation is almost twenty years old. How have things fared since then? Apparently not much has – hah! – changed:

> Would anyone seriously argue we are not living in a period of rapid change? Is it not true that we are also living in an era through which dramatic changes of productivity, technology [etc.] are common-place? (Carnall, 2007: 3)

The questions here are rhetorical, of course. For most authors the idea of being in a specific 'era' of change seems to be self-evident. Open just about any book on organization theory or management and, in one form or another, you will find a similar formulation – almost always on the introductory page.[1] This is partly because many of these texts feed off each other: referencing each other, drawing ideas off each other, looking to each other for supporting evidence. This does not invalidate them, for all discursive formations exhibit this kind of interlocking structure, but it does create a remarkably unchallenged consensus about the 'fact' of change.

And it is not just within organization theory that notions of unprecedented change are invoked. What really marks out the power of the change fetish is the way that it figures in just about every magazine and newspaper article about business, politics and society as a background assumption, as well as in all kinds of training courses and seminars. Whenever I meet managers – or management students, for that matter – I find that, almost without exception, they produce the same mantra: the world is changing at an ever-faster rate and organizations must change in line with it. There have been – recently – a few texts questioning facets of the fetish of change, but only a very few. Certainly, at least for the time being, such questioning is not reflected in the wider literature, still less in popular management texts.

Of course, to describe a world in change might be no more than a rather self-evident comment about the character of human existence. Heraclitus of Ephesus, the Ancient Greek philosopher, suggested that all things are in flux, albeit at different rates, famously pointing out that when you put your foot in a river it immediately ceases to be the same river. Simply by virtue of being in time, change is occurring. But the fetish of change goes much beyond this. First, it conceptualizes current rates of change as unprecedented, and as defining of an era rather than simply being a truism of existence. Second, it ascribes change not to the ineluctable character of time but to certain determinate features, such as technology and globalization. Third, change is envisaged as something amenable to interventions rather than as a spontaneous flux.

The notion of managing change typically refers not to attempts to manage the wider changes of the economy and technology but to attempts to manage organizational responses (whether 'reactive' or 'proactive') to these. In other words, change management refers to attempts by organizations to change themselves in response to actual or predicted environmental change. And such responses are not thought of as being optional: organizations which do not respond adequately to environmental change will not survive in the face of, in particular, competition.

Of course the judgements about what *types* of change must be made in organizations and the methods of achieving these changes will vary according to the situation. In some cases it will be a matter of developing new products, or marketing existing products in a new way. In other cases it will be investment in new technologies; vertical or horizontal integrations; geographical relocations or any number of other things. Despite this diversity, one of the common themes of organizational change in recent years has been changes in organizational design associated with culture management and the assault on bureaucracy.

It is unlikely that there is anyone who has spent any time at all studying organizations or, for that matter, working in them in recent years who has not been exposed to the assumption that change is getting more rapid and is vital to organizational survival. This, I suggest, has become a central part of the common-sense and taken-for-granted knowledge about organizations.

reasons for scepticism

I want now to suggest that there are a number of reasons to be sceptical about common sense in relation to change and change management.

The first issue is that the belief that we live in times of unprecedented change is one which is found in many ages, and perhaps every age. In retrospect the past seems more stable than the present because it is familiar to us and because we experience it in the sanitized and rationalized form of history books or through the haze of nostalgic memory. Yet it is possible to point to any number of periods in the past when, for those alive, it must have seemed as if the world was changing in unprecedented and dramatic ways: the collapse of the Roman Empire; the colonization of the Americas; the Renaissance; the Reformation; the Enlightenment; the Industrial Revolution; the World Wars. The shift from religious to secular conceptions of the world over the last four centuries has, and continues to have, massive ramifications throughout the world, beside which any issues of globalization and technical change experienced in recent years – even accepting these at face value – seem fairly limited.

There is no reason to think that the present time is one of greater change than in the past, or that we are the first people to experience change as being unprecedented. Or, to put it differently and perhaps rather better, there is no *basis* upon which it would be possible to sustain or evaluate such claims. Who is to say that the changes associated with the microchip are faster or more far-reaching than those associated with the printing press? What dimensions of change are we talking about? For whom? Is it possible to attribute causation to particular technologies anyway, given that these are part of a network of social relations which are part and parcel of the inventions and discoveries to which they give rise?

What we do know is that there is a tendency to look back to the past as a 'golden age' now lost by the travails of time. For example, it's familiar how fears about crime show a recurring pattern of beliefs that 'twenty years ago' we lived in a period of stability, order and morality. In terms of organization theory there seems to be, as I said earlier, a belief that there has been a fundamental shift from the 'good old days' of stable bureaucracies, mass markets, Fordism and modernism to the new world of post-bureaucracy, niche markets, post-Fordism and postmodernism. The authorized version of organization theory normally periodizes this in terms of a stable era from 1945 through to the oil crisis of 1974.

Yet in many respects one would hardly classify the post-war order as one of stability, whether economically, politically or technologically. The received wisdom of post-war stability rather conveniently ignores, inter alia, the space race; the development of computers; the Cold War; the arms race; decolonization; the Korean and Vietnam wars; the feminist movement; major waves of immigration and emigration; major shifts in youth culture and the relations between generations. It is not clear that these constituted a 'stable environment'.

Let me shift the analysis for a moment from the general to the personal – and these are by no means separate realms, for the one invariably constitutes the other. In 1945 my late father was an agricultural labourer in Britain. By 1948 he had travelled thousands of miles to work in large-scale mechanized agriculture in Canada. In 1952 he was up to his neck in mud fixing tanks in the Korean War. Around the same time, my late father-in-law was fleeing the Bulgarian secret police hanging beneath the Orient Express from Sofia in mid-winter. After various periods as a prisoner in Tito's Yugoslavia and international camps, he escaped to France – an illegal immigrant with no money, no friends and barely any clothes. I don't think that either of these men would recognize the picture of post-war stability found in the textbooks.

Even the jewel in the crown of the change fetish – increased globalization – is by no means as clear-cut an issue as is commonly supposed. Hirst and Thompson's important (1996) book exposes claims about economic globalization to rigorous and sceptical scrutiny. Comparing the ratio of trade to gross domestic product (GDP), for example, they find that this has dropped in most industrialized countries over the course of the twentieth century, and using a range of measures they claim that 'unequivocally ... openness was more in the Gold Standard period than even in the 1980s' (Hirst and Thompson, 1996: 28). With slightly less confidence, they argue that migration (of people) was substantially less in the twentieth century than the nineteenth, certainly as a proportion of the world's population. Overall, they conclude that 'the international economy was hardly less integrated before 1914 than it is today' (1996: 196–7).

None of this is to say that change does not occur. However, what is at issue is how change is apprehended within particular cultural and historical settings. The key point is that if – as is the case in mainstream contemporary organization theory – we collectively construe our times as being characterized by rapid and unprecedented change, then we are likely, through acting on that belief, to render it self-fulfilling, so that this construction is real in its effects – effects which are discussed in the next chapter. Moreover the generalized claim of 'unprecedented' change is a significant rhetorical device to provoke fear and provide a justification for particular organizational changes. It is necessary, then, to understand the perspectival nature of change: what matters is how we see it, and that depends on where we look from.

the treadmill of change

Organization theory typically looks from, or through, a number of metaphors which have the effect of legitimating the fetish of change. Perhaps the most longstanding is the mechanistic metaphor of the organization as machine. This, in line with the classical approaches I discussed earlier in this book, licenses a vision of the change manager as an engineer, and indeed change management techniques are often described as 'a toolkit'. But in terms of the *justification* of change, the more important metaphor is organismic. This stresses, first, the idea of the organization as distinct from the environment and, second, the necessity of adaptation of the former to the latter.

Such debates leave untouched the fundamental assumption of a boundary between the inside and outside of an organization (a boundary which also allows most organization theory to ignore society, culture, history and philosophy). But where is this boundary? Is it that of the physical premises of an organization? Plainly not, because, for example, networks of supply and distribution affect and are affected by the organization whilst lying outside its physical boundaries. Is it the people employed? Plainly not, because what about customers, shareholders and so on? Insofar as any boundaries can be discerned between an organization and its environment, these are defined through socially and historically specific conventions.

More specifically, organizational boundaries are defined through the deployment of certain bodies of expertise such as law or accounting. Yet these are conventions or constructs. An organization may be able, legally, to regard the locality and community around it as external so that the social costs of laying off workers or polluting the environment (in the ecological sense) are not borne by the organization. However, there is no necessity in this line – it is not 'natural' – since companies could be made to account for externalities and held liable for various effects.

As well as conceiving of organizations as distinct from their environments, common sense, backed up by conventional organizational theory, configures the relationship between the two as a Darwinian one in which those which adapt to the environment survive whilst those which do not are doomed. The Darwinian metaphor is perhaps particularly associated with the population–ecology model of organizations (Aldrich, 1979), although it has come to be used far more widely, and imprecisely, as part of the general vocabulary of management. Interestingly, the strict interpretation of the population–ecology model would suggest there is no scope for management to influence the success or failure of an organization's fit with the environment, and hence its survival, since the environment 'selects' organizations. However, the more general impact of structural contingency and strategic choice theory suggests that a 'fit' between organizations and their environments is something that can be, and is, achieved managerially. Certainly the latter is the *core* assumption of all change management ideas which are necessarily predicated upon the belief that organizations can be managed in ways that 'make a difference' to the capacity of an organization to succeed in its environment.

But I am anticipating what will be discussed more fully later. Returning to organismic metaphors, these are unhelpful because they conceal the sense in which organizations and environments are mutually constitutive. Plainly, the environment of any organization (call it organization A) consists of other organizations, and each of those organizations operates in an environment of which organization A is a part. Organization A is therefore not just part of the environment of *other* organizations, but also part of its *own* environment. This is not to be confused with the proposition that organizations and environments are interdependent: rather it is to say that positing the very notions of organization and environment as separate is misleading.

In less abstract terms, this means that as an organization changes, it contributes to the rationale for change in other organizations, which in turn provide a rationale for change in the original organization. Ultimately this is likely to be futile: suppose an organization implements, for example, total quality management (TQM) for 'the first time in the world' (or for the first time in a particular industry) and further suppose that this yields competitive advantage. Other organizations then seek to adopt TQM and, assuming that all organizations are equally successful in their implementations, the end result will be that no organization has competitive advantage. In short, I am suggesting that organizations collectively generate a 'treadmill' of change which is then seen as a problematic environment to which an organizational response must be made.

It is indeed very obvious that TQM illustrates this point. The 'quality revolution' of the 1980s came to be seen in the 1990s as being inadequate by virtue of its attachment to 'incremental change'. A new 'revolution' was needed and instigated in the form of business process re-engineering (BPR). But BPR then became seen as 'limited', and although the word 're-engineering' is still fairly often used in organizations, the term BPR is now rarely heard. Instead a variety of terminologies such as 'lean' and indeed 'post-bureaucracy' are used to describe the latest turn of the wheel.

Of course, an obvious objection to the treadmill view I am expressing here would be to point out that, although organizations generate change collectively, any individual organization has little choice but to participate if it is to survive. It is here that the Darwinian metaphor comes into play – that survival is contingent upon adaptation because organizations that do not change will lose business to those that do. Yet there are surely reasons to doubt whether this is true. First, it cannot be assumed that organizational change does in fact lead to better or cheaper products (or to greater profitability), and, if it does not, there is no reason to assume that adaptation will be commercially beneficial. Second, even if change does lead to better or cheaper products it does not follow that customers will buy from that organization rather than another. It may be that a less good or more expensive product is compensated for by other considerations such as a particular personal relationship between buyer and seller, or habit, or convenience, or principle, or brand loyalty. To put it another way, there are all sorts of reasons why consumers are not the rational utility-maximizing agents of economic theory.

Anticipating another objection it might be thought that, currently, change programmes are often directed at giving the customer what s/he wants, including all of the 'non-rational' considerations I have just listed. However, changes conducted in the name of the customer may be very far from being the same as changes desired by the customer and may even coexist with monopoly supply of vital services, as with the privatization of some public services. Even where this is not so, many supposedly customer-oriented changes are, in reality, just the opposite. Consider the recent trend towards creating central call centres for dealing with customer enquiries in industries such as banking and insurance. Typically they involve long waits in telephone queues, dealing with elaborate automated menus and finally being connected with an automaton with no personal interest in or knowledge of the customer. In such cases, whilst change is justified in terms of the increasingly demanding nature of customers, the actual practices would seem more animated by a concern to cut costs. As for customer choice, since in many industries (e.g. mobile phones, banks) all the competing companies use these same techniques there is, in that respect, no choice for the customer at all.

In any case, the person of the customer cannot be dissociated from the person of the employee. Thus organizational change programmes which, for example, remove staff in the name of the customer and organizational survival are damaging the capacity of those staff to act as customers and, therefore, the prospects for survival of those organizations relying on this custom. This, of course, is merely another aspect of the inseparability of organizations and environments: the same individual is simultaneously a producer and a consumer. Indeed, one aspect of the recent economic crisis discussed in the next chapter is the way that the offshoring of jobs from developed countries reduced domestic demand, something concealed for a while by increased personal indebtedness but now very obvious as the availability of credit reduces.

My argument in this section is that, far from being a natural, environmental given to which organizations must respond, change is better understood as a construction affected by the interplay (and its unintended consequences) of organizations themselves. To say it is a construct is not to say that it is unreal (and I will discuss some of its effects in the next chapter), but rather that its reality is in part an effect of organizational practices rather than a precursor of those practices. Yet, by constructing a changing world, organizations also create the apparent necessity to 'manage change'. It is to this that I now turn attention.

why change management fails

The most striking thing about change management is that it almost always fails. Despite (or, who knows, because of) the reams of worthy academic treatises, the unending stream of self-congratulatory 'I did it my way' blather from pensioned-off executives and the veritable textual diarrhoea of self-serving guru handbooks, change remains a mystery.

And I do not think that the answer is just around the corner: rather, change management rests upon the conceit that it is possible to systematically control social and organizational relations. But the limits to such a view are very considerable, for the reasons I have tried to explain at several points throughout this book, and will return to again in the Conclusion.

Change management a failure? Is this just wild generalization from an 'armchair critic', perhaps even a 'so-called intellectual'? But Crosby (1979) – a leading advocate of TQM – said that 90 per cent of such projects fail to meet their targets, whilst Stewart (1993) gave a failure figure of 50–70 per cent for BPR projects and Gupta (2005) suggests that 60 per cent of Six Sigma (effectively TQM under a different name) projects fail. It is more difficult to give figures for general change management programmes rather than those badged with labels like TQM and BPR, perhaps one reason why such badgings are less common than in the past. But the general pattern is well-known. New techniques are announced with a great fanfare, and presented as the unproblematic solution to previous problems, but disillusion soon sets in. Some of this is bound up with the marketing activities of consultants and gurus. But there is more to it than that. Managers responsible for particular change programmes are likely, for career and identity reasons, to describe them as successful. Yet the everyday experience of people in organizations is that one change programme gives way to another in a perennially failing operation: nirvana is always just on its way.

In this context, the now massive prescriptive literature of organizational change takes on an interesting aspect. On the one hand, it must always be pointing to the failure of change management (else why the need for this new book?), whilst, on the other hand, never admitting the illusory nature of successful change management (else why the need for any new book?). Much of the conflict stems here from the search for a formula or methodology which promises success in a wide variety of settings. For change management is predicated upon the substitutability of, or generalizability from, what has (supposedly) worked in one situation to another.

We can see here the social practice which underlies the observation I made earlier about the way in which organizations adopting homogeneous 'solutions' to problems in the name of competitive advantage must inevitably end up without such an advantage. For this is not just an anomaly but an inevitable feature of change management. It is most evident in relation to the very common change management methodology of 'benchmarking'. Benchmarking aims to measure and match an organization's existing products and procedures with those of competitors and, in particular, those of organizations perceived to be field leaders. It is part of a process that institutional theorists have described as 'mimetic isomorphism' (DiMaggio and Powell, 1983) or, as we might more straightforwardly say, copying. Benchmarking[2], as a general preparation for the deployment of particular change management techniques in the name of 'best practice', is expressive of the underlying search for generalizability which characterizes change management.

According to a survey of UK Top 1000 companies, 67 per cent of such companies engage in benchmarking (cited in Carnall, 1995: 5). With an amusing circularity, the implication of this, in the context it is cited, is that since benchmarking is common in 'top' companies it should be adopted generally! Yet benchmarking embodies several obvious inanities, even within its own terms. First, there is the issue already alluded to that it can only (at best, assuming 'successful' implementation) lead to equality, not to advantage. Second, and relatedly, it might be thought that if competitive advantage is what is at stake, the thing to emulate would be the process by which an organization comes up with an original basis for innovation, rather than its outcome. Third, it seems well established that today's successful companies are very often tomorrow's failures (as mentioned earlier in this book, consider the later fate of the majority of those companies designated as 'excellent' by Peters and Waterman, 1982). Think of Enron, Arthur Andersen, Marconi, Royal Bank of Scotland, Lehmann Brothers. Yet despite this there is an insatiable demand for, and invincible stupidity about, case studies and stories from such companies and a quite myopic lionization of whatever today's successes are.

But finally, and most significantly, generalizability and hence benchmarking are predicated upon the assumption that organizational settings are homogeneous with respect to the relevant features. In other words, it is assumed that doing what another organization did with a different set of people in a different place at a different time will yield the same results as those claimed for the original implementation. The irony of such an assumption is that, within a discourse obsessed with change, it relies upon everything being the same. And what do such claims amount to anyway? Let's assume an organization is successful in terms of (say) increased profitability following the introduction of (say) a new organizational structure. There is no way of knowing whether this success was because of, despite, or coincidental with, the new structure. It is not known, by definition, whether had another structure been adopted the organization would have been even more profitable. There is no counterfactual, nor could there be.

Indeed, the counterfactual problem is an enduring one for change management – and management generally – irrespective of the benchmarking issue. It is never possible to know what would have happened had a change programme not been introduced, nor which effects can be assigned to which change. This problem is exacerbated by the fact that, in practice, most large organizations run several change programmes simultaneously, and typically embark upon new programmes before the old ones have 'bedded down'. All this makes both success and failure slippery concepts, and whether or not a programme is seen as successful will be an outcome of organizational politics and the context in which the outcome is being debated (for example, organizations may be happy, for public relations reasons, to figure as 'best practice' examples in management texts – the internal perception may be quite different). Finally, on this issue, what constitutes success is crucially, and rather obviously, dependent upon how success is defined and by whom. A successful change management programme from one perspective might be degraded and intensified work conditions from another.

Not only is it difficult – and perhaps in principle impossible – to know whether a change programme has been successful, it is also, to say the least, questionable whether change can be regarded as manageable at all (a parallel argument to that made in the previous chapter about culture management, which of course is one particular variant of change management). Although there are innumerable change models, the issues in this respect are well illustrated by the classic Lewin model (Lewin, 1951) still used as the basis of thinking about organizational change by many, perhaps most, consultants and managers. The basic premise of the received version of this model (I say 'received' because, as with many ideas about organizations which end up as formulaic managerial knowledge, there was more complexity in the original formulation) is that there is a balance of forces which keeps a situation stable and that the task of change management is either to increase the forces for change or decrease the forces against change. Change management thus proceeds in the three steps of unfreezing, moving and refreezing.

The dominant metaphor here is mechanistic: there are 'forces' which operate to stabilize or destabilize an organization. The organization can be unfrozen and refrozen at will. Yet are organizations as amenable to control as (say) a block of ice? And of course this mechanistic view relates to the issue of generalizability. If the manager is a technician who understands the 'physics' of organizational force fields and the 'mechanics' of organizational refrigeration, then plainly this implies a reliable and transferable kind of knowledge. This version of management is, of course, not unique to change but is part and parcel of the engineering model and of the top-down fantasy of managerial omnipotence found within culture management, which grows out of the classical approaches to organizational theory discussed in the first part of this book.

It is worth recapping and extending what I have said so far about why this is a fantasy. It goes back to what I said in Chapter 1 about the project of management in organizations. The core issue is the inherent uncontrollability of social relations. As Roberts (1984), drawing upon the work of the philosopher Alisdair MacIntyre and the sociologist Anthony Giddens, explains, management typically assumes that systematic control of social relations is possible and therefore treats people as if they are simply objects rather than also as subjects. In other words, people are assumed to be passive receivers of others' actions rather than being themselves actors who can (and do) respond differentially to events, interpret them in a differential way and deliberately or unwittingly obstruct and subvert these actions. People are capable of noticing and reflecting upon what goes on around them, and of acting differently, for whatever reason, as a result.

The capacity (and necessity) of people to be both subjects and objects links much of what I have said both in this chapter and throughout this book. It explains why mechanistic understandings of change (and management generally) are so inappropriate. For all the talk of forces and freezing, people do not act in the same way as molecules of water: they act in ways that are both unpredictable but, more importantly, are subject to deliberate and intentional change on the part of the individuals concerned. By the same token, mechanistic understandings underlie the issues of generalizability and the counterfactual problem. If the issue were simply one of freezing and refreezing molecules of water, it would be possible to say that given like conditions, which could readily be replicated, the molecules will behave in the same way. But in organizations like conditions can never – literally *never* – be specified or replicated.

None of this should be reduced to the trite observation that the problem for change management is that 'people are all individuals'. What is at stake here is that people exist within a range of meaning structures (including those, discussed in Chapter 2, that allow people to experience their agency as an individual attribute) of which the organizational is only one. These meaning structures are indeterminate and open-ended, and therefore unpredictable in their effects and likely to give rise to unintended consequences. Nor is the issue here that hardy perennial of the change management literature, 'resistance to change'. Here the suggestion is that people are naturally conservative and when new changes are proposed will inevitably resist them at first, so that the task of the change manager is to work through this resistance until ultimate acceptance is achieved. There is probably not a single prescriptive book on change management which does not make an argument of this sort, but a moment's thought shows that it is nonsense. If the newly proposed change were, say, a pay rise all round, or reduced working hours, does anyone seriously think that there would be inevitable resistance that would have to gradually be overcome? Of course not. The usual reason why change management programmes are resisted is not because of any generalized antipathy to any sort of change, it is because of the particular changes typically sought by such programmes. And it may well also be because those who have been employed for any length of time will have seen the constant cycle of failed change programmes I have discussed here and are, not unreasonably, less than enthusiastic about going through another one.

In this sense, the problems encountered by change management are an aspect of the problems of social science in general. Indeed, much organization theory derives from social science, albeit often in bowdlerized form. Yet, as mentioned earlier, the promise of control derived from social science is illusory. So it should not be thought, as some diehards claim, that going back to social science (even in some more rigorous way than managers have been wont to do) to get better models will solve the problem of control since, in this respect, social sciences are 'almost or perhaps completely devoid of achievement. For the salient fact about these sciences is the absence of any law-like generalisations whatsoever' (MacIntyre, 1981: 88). Indeed, perhaps that is why the most common panacea proposed for the problems of change management is something which has little scientific about it at all, namely quasi-mystical invocations of the need for 'visionary leaders'. In most areas of life we are rightly suspicious of those who have visions. Only in the failed world of change management are they clung to in the desperate hope that they point the way to the promised land.

conclusion

Organization theory may be said to have started with an observation, by Max Weber no less, that the modern world had broken with the past in its preoccupation with the technical efficiency provided by bureaucracy. That observation still seems, with a great deal of hindsight, to be very well founded. Ever since then, there have been endless proclamations of another new era, but these do not seem to be so well founded. I think the post-bureaucracy claim is a case in point. Now of course this kind of thing is difficult to judge. 'History never looks like history when you are living through it. It always looks confusing and messy and it always feels uncomfortable' said John Gardner (in Daintith, 2000: 81). So I may be wrong (but, for the same reasons, the proponents of post-bureaucracy should be wary).

Predictably, I don't think I am wrong, though. I have referred to some empirical evidence that calls the post-bureaucracy thesis into question. However, to be fair, I have also indicated that this kind of argument isn't likely to be settled by empirical evidence given the problems of interpretation. But what may be more important is that I have, I hope, showed that whatever the empirics of organizations, in terms of organization theory there is a very strong continuity which seems to give the lie to this new-era thinking.

For what is striking is not just the repetition of the claims about new organizational forms and the management of change which will bring them into existence, but the repetition of a way of thinking that shows almost no development from the classical approaches to organization theory that I outlined in the first two chapters. For all the talk about new paradigms, contemporary organization theory and managerial method remain remarkably unchanged from their classical roots. Recent techniques associated with 'Toyota-ism', itself a version of post-bureaucratic thinking, show precisely the same preoccupations as those found in Fordism: the much-documented Toyota–General Motors initiative at the NUMMI plant in California ensured that workers who had previously averaged 45 seconds work in the minute now work for 57 seconds (Basso, 2003: 64). Frederick Taylor's stopwatch has hardly been consigned to the pages of organization theory textbooks. More generically, the underlying philosophy of instrumental rationality and control remains firmly in the ascendant in post-bureaucracy. This means that the post-bureaucratic revolution is extremely unlikely to succeed, but it also means that, even if it were to succeed, it would only initiate an even more intensive and even less morally defensible subjugation of human potentiality.

And even if you do not accept this, consider another striking fact. All of the talk about change and ripping up bureaucracy, is itself quite remarkably unchanging. The same generalized claims about being in a new era of change are made decade after decade, the same organizational prescriptions of visionary leadership and overcoming resistance are made decade after decade, the same confident faith in change management is trumpeted decade after decade as if, this time, things will be different. So it seems as if one thing, at least, is immune from change: wheeling out the same old stuff about change and the imminent end of bureaucracy. One reason for this is that, despite its critics, bureaucracy does have some virtues of efficiency and fairness, and so persists. Another is that bureaucracy is the pantomime villain of organization theory, the bogeyman which never disappears. A third is that often the changes introduced as 'post-bureaucratic' turn out to be bureaucracy under a new name.

Does this mean that all this talk of post-bureaucracy and change can just be ignored? Unfortunately not. For there can be no doubt that they have exerted a considerable hold over the managerial imagination. In organizations, the kind of organization theory I have discussed in this chapter enjoys a remarkable ascendancy and this is most obvious, because it attracts most media attention, in public sector organizations. At least in the UK, almost every government policy is predicated on the assumptions of post-bureaucracy, sometimes explicitly using this term and almost invariably invoking the mantra of change – and again this has been true for at least three decades, if not longer. The current British Prime Minister explicitly champions post-bureaucracy as *the* solution to public service provision (Cameron, 2010). It is assumed that public services must be purged of bureaucracy and that the economy must change to be able to compete in a globalized knowledge economy. And it is assumed that what matters in policy is 'what works' – in other words, the instrumental rationality of organization theory has been taken up as a political philosophy. Once again, the boundary between organization theory and other arenas is a fuzzy one but, in this case, rather than import political issues into organization theory, politics has adopted the dubious nostrums of managerial versions of organization theory.

In doing so, I believe that politicians – like business leaders – have used organization theory in precisely the way that, in the Introduction to this book, I claimed that theory is always used: as a weapon to pursue particular agendas. The most powerful weapon is the theory of an era of unprecedented change since this can be used to generate compliance, often fearful compliance. Not just this but all these claims about post-bureaucracy and change are really an exercise of power. Anyone who questions them is automatically painted as retrograde, old-fashioned, elitist, resistant to change and, fundamentally, out of step with the modern world. Change is a crass theology, but a theology it is. It is the doctrinal orthodoxy of those who rule us. Be insufficiently worshipful of its doctrine and you will be punished. Inflexibility, 'irrational' resistance to change, not buying in to the vision: these are the new heresies. But this theology is but one aspect of a wider set of issues in the study of organizations, and it is to these that I will now turn.

notes

1 As I implied earlier, these claims recur, always believing themselves to be new. Thus Parker could comment, well over thirty years ago, that '[t]wo accepted clichés about contemporary societies are that they are

experiencing unprecedented rates of change and that they have been drawn together by trade and mass communications into a global village' (1977: 172). Jacques (1996) notes how many of the claims about a second industrial revolution in the late twentieth century are almost identical to those made in the early part of the century. Yet those earlier periods are recast as being *stable* in later accounts.

2 Despite its use within post-bureaucratic discourse, the very word 'benchmarking' is, literally, an engineering term.

5

The New Capitalism and the Strange Fates of Management

*Well, remember that what an ideology is, is a conceptual frame-
work with the way people deal with reality. Everyone has one.
You have to – to exist, you need an ideology. The question is
whether it is accurate or not. And what I'm saying to you is, yes,
I've found a flaw. I don't know how significant or permanent it
is. But I've been very distressed by that fact.*

Alan Greenspan

I indicated in the previous chapter that we need to be very wary of the
extravagant, generalized claims of those who proclaim a new and
unprecedented era of change within which organizations exist and to
which they must respond. Such 'epochal thinking' (du Gay, 2003) with
its 'cartoon concepts' (Froud et al., 2006: 66) such as post-bureaucracy
is at best over-simplified and at worst acts to justify punitive assaults on
people's lives and livelihoods. However, it would be equally flawed to
claim that, somehow, nothing changes or has changed and to fail to
understand organizations within their wider cultural and economic context. But 'context' is far too anaemic a word: organizations are both
a cause and consequence of, and so inseparable from, culture and
economics.

In this chapter I want, to a greater extent than I have before, to locate
the study of organizations within this inseparability. Of course to do this
fully would require much more space than I can devote to it – several
long books, in fact – so I am going to concentrate on some contemporary issues about the kind of society and economy that has emerged over
recent decades in the West. Apart from introducing these issues, I also
want to underscore what has been a major theme of this book: that
when we study organizations we must necessarily be concerned with

politics, economics, history and society. It is a major failing of most courses on organizations that they, and knowledge about them, are presented in a way which is denuded of such things, except perhaps in the form of a few trite claims and unstated assumptions. But that failing is part and parcel of treating the study of organizations as a 'technical' matter of delivery, rather than probing the question of what is delivered and why.

the making of the new capitalism

One way of understanding these 'contextual' issues is in terms of what Richard Sennett (1998; 2006) calls 'the new capitalism'. This is a useful term because it reminds us that what is at stake is not some epochal rupture with the past, in the way claimed by the change fetishists: it represents in some ways a continuation of capitalism. On the other hand, the term 'new capitalism' allows us to raise questions about it without falling into an equally useless binary, that of capitalism versus communism – for what is at stake is a particular form of capitalism and its consequences. The new capitalism has many aspects, including the relentless accent upon change and post-bureaucracy discussed in the last chapter. It is manifest in a whole variety of ways including the growing dominance of finance, both in the sense of the global banking and derivatives industries (Stein, 2010) and in the sense of corporate financialization (Folkman et al., 2006; Froud et al., 2006). This latter term carries two meanings. One is the idea that the sole purpose of organizations is the maximization of shareholder value, with businesses having no wider obligations or accountability. The other is the idea that even for firms in the manufacturing sector, a central activity is the use of its assets for purposes of 'financial engineering'. In pursuit of financialization, companies offshore and outsource their activities to countries with the cheapest labour and the most limited protections for employment rights, seeking to 'sweat' their assets – both human and financial – to the maximum extent. Meanwhile, companies themselves are traded and re-traded between investors with little or no long-term interest in them (see Das, 2011 for a readable insider's account of how this financialized new capitalism works).

One of the many organizational consequences of all this is to break the connection between businesses, places and communities. Until relatively recently, the names of organizations often reflected such links. Banks and building societies were, in the UK, called things like the

Midland or the Halifax or the Bradford and Bingley. Airlines were national flag carriers for their countries and were, normally, nationally owned. And company names reflected not just place but function: they were gas firms or water firms, for example. That naming has either changed or become meaningless. Thus Midland is subsumed into HSBC, Halifax into HBOS and subsequently Lloyds. Bradford and Bingley is owned by the huge Spanish financial conglomerate Santander. Airline ownership is largely dispersed: they now rarely have a connection with the country they reference, or have names which don't reference a country at all (Virgin, EasyJet, etc.). Thames Water and Yorkshire Power belong to a German company, RWE; Cadbury's belongs to Kraft; the British Airports Authority belongs to the Spanish firm Ferovial; British Gas is owned by Centrica. British names such as HP sauce, Beefeater Gin, P&O, Weetabix, Jaguar, Rolls-Royce, Hamley's, OXO, The Body Shop, Bass beer, even Harry Ramsden's Fish and Chips shops – and hundreds of others – are now owned by international companies or consortia[1]. Those interested in football (personally I've never been able to get into it) might wish to consider the way that football clubs – at least the elite clubs like Manchester United and Chelsea – now have little connection either in their ownership, their players or their fan base with the localities to which their names bear testament.

The takeover of Cadbury's confectionary by Kraft, mentioned above, is a particularly clear example of how the new capitalism works. This was a firm with a history dating back to the nineteenth century and marked by a strong interest in worker welfare. In 2009 a hostile takeover bid from Kraft, a giant US food corporation, was rejected but subsequently, in 2010, a deal was agreed. The deal generated an estimated £240 million in fees for the investment banks and advisers involved (Blackhurst, 2010). One especially controversial aspect is that Cadbury's had had plans to close its factory in Somerset and move production to Poland, but Kraft undertook that this would not happen if they took over. However, after the takeover the factory was closed in favour of the Polish location, and amongst the hundreds laid off were families who had worked for Cadbury's for decades (Kelly, 2011). So here a workplace rooted in a history and a community was eviscerated. Is this just 'the way things are'? No, because such situations arise from particular regulatory regimes and, as the former chairman of Cadbury's has argued, the UK regulation of overseas takeovers is especially lax (Wearden, 2010).

This isn't a nostalgic, nationalistic lament, nor is it parochialism. Rather, I use these examples because Britain has, indeed, been especially willing to see its companies sold off and this is because, in a sense, just as Britain was in the vanguard of the industrial revolution, so too – along with, in particular, the USA – it was one of the first developed economies to embrace the new capitalism. It has certainly been one of the most enthusiastic adherents of a new capitalist economy based upon financial services, financial engineering, offshoring and outsourcing. But as I will indicate below, similar and related things have occurred in many other countries.

The relaxed attitude to the internationalization of ownership of what were once UK companies reflects a distinctive attitude to organizations. Understood merely as 'brands', ownership doesn't really matter – indeed, many of the brands I have alluded to continue to exist, even though their ownership has changed. But understood as the products of organizations, it most certainly does. The link between ownership, work and community is a complex one, which the language of brands fails to account for. A localized employer, rooted in an area with a workforce that has long-standing personal and familial ties with that product and that employer, is an important source of community. Once the link is broken, then not only are workplace practices likely to change but so too is the meaning of work itself. So too is the meaning of ownership: why should a dispersed, international ownership 'care' about a business above and beyond its financial value? So too is the relationship between business and politics: can individual governments regulate such organizations or must they rather compete to attract them?

Of course there have always been takeovers and mergers of companies, but within the new capitalism companies are traded and re-traded endlessly so that there is never a moment of stability in which ownership patterns settle down. There is an endless reshuffling of the corporate card deck, as if the players of a game of Monopoly were not only suffering from attention deficit disorder but were also taking amphetamines. And remember that what is being traded isn't cards, it isn't even brands – it is the lives and livelihoods of the people who work for these companies. These are the chips being played with in what the late Susan Strange evocatively described as the 'casino capitalism' which emerged from the wholesale deregulation of financial markets in the 1980s (Strange, 1986; see also Das, 2011).

The transformation of the corporate landscape to one of freewheeling globalized financial deals is part and parcel of what the Australian writers Gee et al. (1996) persuasively call the 'fast capitalist story', in which constant transformation of organizations, and constant speeding up of work within those organizations, is mandatory to organizational survival in ways that clearly echo my discussion of post-bureaucracy and change in Chapter 4. In calling it a 'story' they do not mean that it is untrue, but rather that it is an ideology with real effects: that is, to the extent that the story is accepted and acted upon, then the consequences will be real for organizations and individuals who are not 'fast enough', and they will be *punitive*. Gee et al.'s analysis is consistent with a rash of related observations made by several influential commentators on the nature of contemporary society and capitalism, such as Edward Luttwak (1999), who popularized the now widely used term 'turbo-capitalism' to denote these developments, and Boltanski and Chiapello's (2007) analysis of 'the new spirit of capitalism'. Whilst all of the works I have referred to in this paragraph are nuanced in different ways, use different terminologies and have different modes of explanation, they are all, I think, circling a similar set of issues to that which Richard Sennett calls the new capitalism.

Sennett (2006: 37–41) himself locates these developments in the unleashing of huge amounts of investment capital following the collapse of the Bretton Woods Agreement (the system which had regulated international trade and currency movements since the end of the Second World War) in the 1970s. This in turn led to a period of massive restructuring through mergers and acquisitions. Stability, indeed, became seen as a sign of weakness and companies had 'to look beautiful in the eyes of the passing voyeur [by] demonstrating signs of internal change and flexibility' (Sennett, 2006: 40). One might say that the display of this beauty became one of the 'symbols' of the economy of disorganized capitalism identified by Lash and Urry (1994). Such a capitalism is no longer primarily concerned with the production of useful goods and services, but is rather about the promulgation of brands and the pursuit of 'value'.

At the same time as the collapse of the Bretton Woods Agreement was beginning to have effects, a new kind of political analysis was emerging, especially in the UK and the USA, in reaction to the post-Second World War settlement. Inspired by the Chicago School economics of Milton Friedman and a (highly partial) reading of the eighteenth-century economist Adam Smith, this has become known as neo-liberalism, and its basic precepts are that individuals are rational self-interested actors, markets are the best allocator of resources, and the state is both inefficient and immoral in restraining individuals and markets. Translated into policy, this meant deregulation of the private sector, privatization of – or creation of internal markets within – the public sector, breaking the power of trade unions and promoting global free trade. In the USA this agenda informed the 1980s' governments of Ronald Reagan, in the UK those of Margaret Thatcher.

Prophetically, the very first policy decision of the 1979 Thatcher government was the abolition of exchange controls which limited the flows of capital into and out of the UK. And although for many students now these names and dates will seem almost prehistoric, it's important to understand that the basic agenda initiated at this time was accepted by subsequent administrations in those countries up to the present day (see e.g. Heffernan, 2001). Moreover, it had a huge impact on the economic policies of just about every country on the globe, especially following the collapse of the Soviet Union which seemed to imply not just that capitalism was the only game in town but, moreover, that neo-liberal or new capitalism was that game. Of course there is much more to neo-liberalism than this (see Steger and Roy, 2010 for an accessible introduction; Crouch, 2011 for where we are now). It's really impossible to understand organizations in today's world without having some grasp of neo-liberal ideas and policies.

the crisis of the new capitalism

Early indications that something might be rotten at the heart of the new capitalism came with the well-publicized case of the US company Enron. Roberts and Armitage (2006) depict Enron as having developed, since its foundation in 1985, from being a 'modern' organization, specializing in gas distribution, to a 'hypermodern' organization by the end of the twentieth century. As a hypermodern organization, its business became ever more diversified and moved away from being based upon tangible assets, such as gas pipelines, to being a complex web of financial engineering and brand management. In this way, Enron may be said to exemplify Lash and Urry's (1994) insights into disorganized capitalism, in which physicality (actually producing 'things') gives way to an economy of symbolic manipulation ('leveraging the brand'). Enron was in a continuous and continual process of reorganization; work practices were constantly changing, staff turnover was massive. It was lauded as exactly the kind of innovative firm that summed up the supposed virtues of the new capitalism. In 2001 Enron collapsed, mired in a scandal which also destroyed its auditor, Arthur Andersen – then one of the leading global accounting firms which, not coincidentally, shared many organizational features with Enron (Grey, 2003).

Despite this high profile corporate disaster, few at the time were willing to see it as anything other than an anomaly, something caused by the greed and corruption of individuals rather than indicative of any wider systemic problem. Some were more far-sighted. For example, the respected business journalist Simon Caulkin (2007) discussed developments at ICI, one of the world's leading pharmaceutical companies. He pointed out that its global dominance was built on investment in long-term – meaning decades of – research and development work. Yet, under the impact of pressure to conform to the business model of the new capitalism, ICI had transformed itself into a company concerned with deal-making – mergers, demergers, acquisitions, divestments – and the whole panoply of what Caulkin called '… the approved nostrums of financial management … the institutionalised bad management of the kind that ticks all the boxes of the narrow playmakers by whose rules the UK's corporate economy now runs' (Caulkin, 2007). In other words, rather than being an organization to allow the gradual, long-term building of real products, Caulkin saw ICI as becoming a shell for the rapid, short-term generation of shareholder value.

Others were prescient in identifying the deepest flaw within the new capitalism: it is predicated upon massive personal, corporate and state indebtedness. For example, in 2006 the economist Ann Pettifor wrote these prophetic words:

> This book foresees a time, in the not too distant future, when the so-called First World will be mired in … debt. (Pettifor, 2006: 1)

Similarly, Elliott and Atkinson (2007) identified the 'Fantasy Island' economics which had developed in the UK by that date. That is, it is an economy built upon individual consumer spending, which in turn was built upon debt, which in turn was based upon rising house prices which were themselves financed through debt. In 2007 personal debt in the UK for the first time exceeded the annual GDP of that country, and most of the consumption it financed was imported from abroad and in particular from China. In contrast, China and some other countries were running huge budget surpluses and thus, in effect, lending developed nations the money to buy their industrial output. But of course it was not just in the UK that this was happening. In more extreme form, a similar process was under way in the USA in the so-called sub-prime mortgage market (or, more piquantly, 'Ninja' mortgages for those with 'no income, no job and no assets').

Even more precariously, these loans were being packaged up by investments banks into complicated financial instruments which were then used as the basis to leverage further borrowing. The fragility of all of this and the way in which it fell spectacularly apart is now well-known and has been described very fully elsewhere (see Lanchester, 2010 and Tett, 2010 for readable but incisive accounts; Reinhart and Rogoff, 2009 and Engelen et al., 2011 for more detailed academic analysis). A few key events of this debacle include Northern Rock, the UK bank with some of the greatest exposure to sub-prime mortgage debt, which collapsed and was nationalized in February 2008. The Royal Bank of Scotland, in large part due to a disastrous debt-funded takeover, was effectively nationalized the following October. Meanwhile, in the USA, Lehman Brothers, an iconic investment bank, collapsed in September 2008 whilst in the same month the massive US insurance company AIG was in effect nationalized to prevent its collapse. These of course were only a few of the highest profile failures in the financial sector.

So familiar is all of this to us now that it is worth recalling that almost until the moment that the financial crisis happened, the model of the new capitalism from which it grew was enthusiastically espoused by most business leaders, economists and politicians. Gordon Brown, the then British Prime Minister, in his Mansion House speech of 2007, not only lauded the ingenuity and creativity of the City of London, but saw it as providing a template for how Britain and other developed countries should structure other areas of activity and the harbinger of a 'new world order'. Whilst I am making a political point here, it is not one of narrow 'party politics' (indeed it is vital to understand that the main political parties in the UK share in these respects the same ideology). For example, in 2006 George Osborne, now the Conservative Chancellor of the Exchequer, heaped praise on the Irish 'Celtic Tiger' economy, urging its financial deregulation as a model for others to follow. And of course within two years that economy was in tatters and its main banks effectively bankrupt. Pointing these things out is not, or not simply, an exercise in point-scoring. It matters because it shows how comprehensively accepted was the culture of the new capitalism. Though it is easy for people now to pontificate knowingly about 'flawed business models' and 'inadequate regulation', not only did they largely fail to do so at the right time but also, as I will suggest later, the flawed thinking espoused before the financial crisis has by no means disappeared as a result of subsequent events. At the very least, the way in which the new capitalism was presented as unquestionable common sense might embolden us to be more sceptical about current and future claims about what *is* unquestionably common sense. Especially, perhaps, when made by the very same people.

That aside, the ramifications of the financial crisis continue to be felt and, indeed, there is every reason to think that there will be further such crises. There are still not billions but trillions of dollars' worth of obscure financial derivatives in the system, and there is every chance of further banking collapses[2]. In the meantime, what began as a private banking crisis has become a sovereign debt crisis – that is to say a crisis of national indebtedness. In many ways this has come about either directly or indirectly because of the financial crisis. Directly, to the extent that states had to bail out banks in order to prevent their complete collapse and the massive social and economic dislocation which would have followed. It is important to remember this because some free-market ideologues are now claiming that the problem was that of state intervention, and that all would have been well had the banks been allowed to fail. But it is not that policymakers at the time, such as the then US President George W. Bush, had a sudden conversion to socialism. It is that the limits of the free-market theory they espoused had become so obvious that there was no other realistic option. Equally, it is sometimes now said that because the government deficits are higher than the actual money spent on bailouts then 'therefore' these deficits are not mainly attributable to the financial crisis. But this misses the indirect effects of the financial crisis, namely that it caused a global recession, inevitably depressing tax revenues whilst causing increased spending on benefits and so causing spiralling state budget deficits.

And there are other, more complex, connections between financial and sovereign debt crises. Greece is (at the time of writing) the EU country perhaps hardest hit by the sovereign debt crisis, yet it was relatively uninvolved in the global banking crisis. On the other hand, the fact that it was able to get into so much debt in the first place was partly due to its use of complex financial derivatives to conceal the extent to which it had become indebted, and its adviser in this matter was one of the biggest global investment banks, Goldman Sachs (Balzli, 2010). The financial engineering of the new capitalism was not just something done by companies: whole nations were doing it.

Another important connection between the banking crisis and the sovereign debt crisis is the role played by the world's three major credit rating agencies. These agencies, it should be recalled, approved the worthless packages of sub-prime debt as having a 'triple A' credit status and so bear a considerable responsibility for the financial crisis (Asia Development Bank Institute, 2010). Now they have become important players in assessing the creditworthiness of countries, making almost daily pronouncements on this, even though they have no democratic accountability (Kettle, 2010). Whilst purporting merely to 'report' risk to lenders, they also have a role in creating self-fulfilling prophecies because as they downgrade the credit ratings of countries, the cost of those countries' borrowing rises, making them more likely to default on their debts and so worsening their credit rating. From a policy point of view, this places elected governments in a near-impossible position. If they seek to reduce deficits by cutting public expenditure and/or increasing taxes, as has happened in all major Western economies since the financial crisis, then their lack of growth prospects makes their capacity to service their debt reduce and their credit rating is threatened. If they seek to borrow more in order to invest and promote economic growth then their debt levels are seen as unsustainable and their credit rating is threatened. In effect, although the globalization of markets arose largely as the result of decisions taken by sovereign states, those states are now subservient to globalized markets, posing major challenges for democratic accountability. It seems likely that any solution will involve extensive co-operation between states to redress the imbalance of power and, I would think, some eventual partial write-off of sovereign debt, as has occurred in the case of Greece. At the time of writing (March 2012), and especially in the Eurozone countries of Europe, it remains unclear whether or how these issues can be addressed and what consequences will follow if they are not, but the head of the International Monetary Fund, Christine Lagarde, has warned not simply of recession but of a global *depression* on the scale of the 1930s.

The Eurozone crisis has a number of causes, of course, but it shows that the new capitalism is not simply a phenomenon of the USA and the UK, the countries most closely associated with the 'Anglo-Saxon' model. Other countries adopted many of its features in terms of deregulation and a heavy emphasis on financial services and property speculation, Ireland and Spain being two prominent examples. Iceland, outside the European Union, perhaps deserves particular mention. Here, following bank privatization in 2001, a massive wave of lending and borrowing was unleashed and by 2008 both the banks and the country were bankrupt. A whole country had been ruined by the new capitalism in less than a decade. Iceland is also interesting as, following a referendum in 2011, it became what is so far the first country to, in effect, default on its debts as a result of the financial crisis (see Business Insider, 2011 for a clear account of the story of the financial crisis in Iceland).

Beyond this, even though countries like France and, in particular, Germany, Switzerland and the Scandinavian states stood somewhat outside the 'Anglo-Saxon' model, many of their banks – and especially those of France, Germany and Switzerland – were hugely enmeshed within, and affected by, the financial crisis. The reality is that the world financial system is so interconnected that the new capitalism transcended the economic policy models of different countries and so the financial and economic crisis that has unfolded since 2007 is a crisis of pretty much the entire Western world.

▬▬▬ organization studies and the new capitalism

I have provided this very brief overview of recent economic and political events because it is important to see that there is a near seamless connection between these events and work organizations. This can be perceived at many different levels. The investment banks which are at the heart of the crisis are themselves organizations, of course, where the decisions and risks were taken which had such calamitous consequences. For example, the kind of gung-ho, aggressive, deal-making organizational culture that gave the then chief executive of the Royal Bank of Scotland, Fred 'the Shred' Goodwin, his nickname seems to epitomize the wider culture of the new capitalism (the 'shredding' referring to the ruthless cost-cutting that was his trademark). Similarly, Dick Fuld, chief executive of Lehman Brothers up to its demise, earned the nickname 'the Gorilla' as testament to his aggressive and competitive character. Again it is important to recall how, right up to the moment of their downfall, these kinds of business leaders were lionized. Goodwin was knighted for his services to banking and had been, amongst other things, European Banker of the Year in 2003; by 2009 he had become a figure of public derision and hatred and in 2012 was stripped of his knighthood. Likewise, Fuld in 2006 won an award for being the top private-sector chief executive in the USA; in 2008 he received another accolade, being named as the worst American chief executive of all time. I mention these rapid changes in fortune not simply for reasons of *schadenfreude*, but as a caution about the way that currently dominant business leaders who often display similar characteristics of bombast are still treated with reverence and awe – not least by students of business. One thing we might learn from the financial crisis is to be a little less starry-eyed about such people.

Clearly there is more to financial organizations than the personalities of their leaders, and there seems every reason to think that many of these organizations, especially in investment banking, have been characterized by highly aggressive and competitive cultures. In a way these organizations embodied the spirit of the new capitalism: the individualistic, financially-driven, winner-takes-all and lunch-is-for-wimps ethos of neo-liberalism. Many have noted how such organizations seem to valorise a kind of masculinist, testosterone-fuelled behaviour – whether on the part of men or women, though many of the organizations in question are also male-dominated – and if the dealing rooms of the investment banks are the clearest expression of it, the general orientation is evident in many of the workplaces of the new capitalism. Detailed academic study of, specifically, financial traders is unfortunately quite rare (Fenton-O'Creevey et al., 2005 and Stark 2009 being some exceptions) but it seems highly likely that alongside the general economic and political causes of the crisis of new capitalism there are some specifically organizational causes to be found.

But of course the significance of new capitalism for organizations goes beyond the organization of banking. It affected organizations of all sorts. In particular, the financial demands for ever-greater profits in shorter and shorter time frames impacts directly upon how organizations conduct themselves, and the experience of employees within them and of their customers. A good example is that of Southern Cross, the private equity owned firm which managed hundreds of old people's care homes in the UK and collapsed in 2011. Essentially what they had done was, rather than simply to seek a profit from selling their care home services, to sell the properties and then rent them back, whilst using the sale proceeds to invest in other acquisitions. When the rents became unaffordable and the investment portfolio slumped, the whole thing fell apart in a prime example of the follies of financial engineering. This might almost be a case study in what Simon Caulkin (2007), referred to earlier, meant by the institutionalized bad management that is emblematic of the flaws of new capitalist organizations.

A different kind of example is that of Bombardier, the last train-making company in Britain, which in 2011 failed to win a £1.6 billion government contract that went instead to a German rival. Bombardier had its origins in the state-owned British Rail Engineering works, privatized in 1989, later run by a Swiss–Swedish consortium, then by Chrysler, then finally sold to the Canadian firm Bombardier. With each sell off, 'the workforce has shrunk time and again, and the firms supplying it have dwindled too [in a] story of long-running underinvestment' (Chakrabortty, 2011). Again this is a microcosm of hundreds of other companies' stories of constantly churning global ownership and its effects on long-term investment, stability or commitment[3]. This is the organizational consequence of the 'financialization' that leads to an 'economy of permanent restructuring' (Froud et al., 2006). The social consequences of such an economy are to make it 'rootless': unconnected with places or communities. Richard Sennett's (1998) research is very revealing on this point. Based upon studies of several individuals and groups of workers (including some whom he had studied twenty years previously), he argues that it is the radical disorganization of work associated with the new capitalism which has disoriented and even destroyed what had previously been reasonably solid social relations. In particular, the erosion of stable career structures, where the work ethic was rewarded and which existed within reasonably secure organizations embedded within communities, has been a major factor in eroding trust and well-being. There is really no line that can be drawn between issues of organization, economics, society and politics.

Similarly, one important consequence of the financial crisis has been to expose much more forcibly how organizations within the new capitalism were marked by massive increases in inequality. In the UK, the High Pay Commission reported in 2011 that in the period since 1980, average annual earnings had risen from £6,474 to £25,900, a real increase of 300 per cent. But in the same period the pay of top executives had increased by 4000 per cent (High Pay Commission, 2011a: 7). This meant that, within individual organizations – organizations where, to recall what I wrote in the previous two chapters, all the talk at the time had been of shared purpose and flattened hierarchies – the ratio between the highest and lowest paid was increasing dramatically. The High Pay Commission gave some examples, and I will take one from the manufacturing sector and one from the financial sector. At British Petroleum in 1979–80 top pay was 16.5 times higher than the average wage in the company; in 2009–2011 it was 63.2 times higher. At Barclays Bank, in 1979–80 the multiple was 14.5; in 2009–2011 it was 75. Neither of these is the largest example of the growth in pay inequality within organizations. And even during the current economic recession the picture is the same, so that in the year up to the report, the average pay of employees in FTSE-100 companies rose by 2.9 per cent, whilst that of executives rose by 49 per cent (all figures quoted from High Pay Commission, 2011a: 9).

Unsurprisingly, this growth in pay inequality maps on to a growth in overall economic inequality (because most people's economic position depends on paid employment), and not just in the UK. In 2011 the OECD produced a major report showing how inequality had risen in 17 out of the 22 OECD countries for which figures were available since the mid-1980s, and within those the five countries which were both the most unequal and in which inequality had risen during the period were (in order of the most unequal): Mexico, the USA, Israel, the UK and Italy (OECD, 2011: 24). Inequality has many organizational consequences as well as causes, the most basic being the way it feeds understandings of unfairness. Perhaps if executive pay was clearly related to performance that would be less true – but, as explored later, it is not. Inequality also has many social consequences, on health, on crime, on civility and on general well-being, not just for the poorest but for the richest too, as the influential work of Wilkinson and Pickett (2010) has persuasively shown. In brief, societies where economic equality is greater tend to be happier, healthier and more harmonious. Here again we can see the unavoidable connection between organizations and society, a connection which makes it indefensible to try to study the former without studying the latter.

Apart from growing inequality, what also now stands brutally exposed is how insecure the new capitalism has made most of us, and again much of that insecurity is organizational (see Boltanski and Chiapello, 2007). Even as security, in the sense of protection of the population from terrorism, has become a central policy issue for governments, security, in the economic sense, has diminished. Stable employment is for most people the central plank of economic security, but that has diminished because the post-bureaucratic organizations of the new capitalism offer no such stability. And whilst that might not have seemed to matter too much before the financial crisis, now the spectre of rising unemployment makes this insecurity real. Most people in the UK are apocryphally said to be just three pay cheques away from homelessness. In many countries, pensions – which used to be a central part of the security provided by employment – are under severe pressure, where they exist at all. Education no longer guarantees a well-paid job and, at university level, is increasingly expensive. And so the social contract which has obtained in Western democracies[4] for at least seventy years – which said that if you took advantage of the education offered by the state and worked reasonably hard then you could expect to have secure employment and a secure old age, and would be protected by welfare if things went wrong with your health or some other piece of bad luck – is breaking up. Organizations and more particularly work were the central part of that social contract and as they retreat from that, so is emerging a new 'precariat' – the term coined by Standing (2011) combining the words 'precarious' and 'proletariat'.

What is at stake is not something minor, with people feeling 'a bit worried'. The destruction of security threatens to rip up individual and social life. Again, Greece is a good example because it has been so forcefully exposed to the consequences of the collapse of the new capitalism. Pensioners there are in desperation, youth unemployment is currently 36 per cent and rising, crime is rising, even suicide rates have risen by 40 per cent in a year (Smith, 2011a; 2011b). And whilst Greece may be the most extreme example, the same picture is evident across Europe. In other words, entire countries and entire generations within countries are being destroyed as the consequences of the crisis of the new capitalism are playing out.

Within such a scenario there are huge dangers, which are already beginning to emerge. Even the most cursory knowledge of history tells us that severe economic crisis begets intolerance and worse towards marginal groups. Thus we already see increasing racism in Europe. Moreover, we see people turning on each other so that those in work perceive 'welfare scroungers' as the problem; those employed in the private sector

see public sector workers as parasites; the young see the older generation as having taken all the benefits and left them with debts and no
prospects. All of these divisions are beside the point though. The forty-
year experiment in new capitalism has, as indicated above, initiated a
massive inequality between rich and poor and it is this cleavage, rather
than those amongst the relatively poor, which is surely the most significant. What was, in Western countries anyway, an accumulated 'common
wealth' has been sold off to the benefit of a small global elite and to the
detriment of everyone else. Indeed on one estimate, just 737 entities
(e.g. banks, multinational companies) control 80 per cent of the world's
capital (Vitali et al., 2011). It is not that the security of the past has
become magically 'unaffordable', it is not that this or that group of
workers or benefit claimants has become enriched, so pointing the finger
of blame at such groups is misconceived. For example, in the UK benefit
fraud amounted to about £22 million in 2010 (Department for Social
Development, 2011), but UK tax evasion[5] amounted to just under
£70 *billion* (Tax Justice Network, 2011) which, apart from being massively greater than benefit fraud, represents over half the cost of the
National Health Service! Even supposing that these estimates are significantly wrong, and by definition they are prone to error, order of
magnitude and hence the overall picture is very clear (see Murphy, 2011
for substantial detail on the issue of tax evasion). But even without tax
evasion – which is, after all, illegal – an entirely legalized transfer of
wealth is what has eroded the security of the majority. Almost all of us
have been quietly mugged over the last forty years.

This kind of analysis has been not just articulated but physically
manifested in the burgeoning popular reaction to the financial crisis. In
particular, the Occupy Movement and the related Indignant Movement,
with their street protests in New York, London, Madrid and many other
places rallied around the slogan of 'the 99%' – meaning the vast majority
as opposed to the 1 per cent who benefit from the new capitalism. Stupid
people have queried what this 'statistic' refers to, but its meaning is clear
enough: the vast majority have been shafted; a tiny minority have benefitted. Others have criticized these movements for failing to articulate alternatives, as if the present system had some fully-worked out justification
of itself, or could provide one. That is to say, no one set out a blueprint
for current society in the way demanded of the protestors for future society; at most, societal arrangements flow from broad principles.

What has the study of organizations to contribute to all this? I think
the answer is 'quite a lot' because work and its organization is so central
both to what has been lost and to what could be reclaimed. It seems to
me that there is much more that organization studies as an academic
discipline could and should do, though. Much of the research in the field

is, not unsurprisingly and not unreasonably, concerned with existing organizations. What is much less common – actually, all but non-existent – is any attempt to articulate alternative organizational forms to those we currently have. One project is under way in this regard, but it has not yet reported (Parker et al., forthcoming in 2013, but see in the meantime Parker et al., 2007). But at all events, the new capitalist model of organizations is most certainly not the only one available. Co-operatives and mutuals formed the bedrock of nineteenth-century working-class reactions to the inequalities and insecurities of the day, including the mutual building societies which provided home loans and savings accounts, initially for particular towns and regions. It is ironic that many of those which were most successful and survived into the 1980s were then privatized and have now disappeared. In fact, *every single* mutual building society which privatized no longer exists, which says something about the false promise of the new capitalism. But some of the smaller mutuals are still there whilst, at a much bigger level of operations, the Co-operative Wholesale Society has a thriving network of shops and other services. Even more successful is the John Lewis Partnership and its supermarket subsidiary Waitrose. It is bizarre, then, that when the Co-operative Bank was named as preferred bidder to take on parts of the branch network of Lloyds Bank, one of those bailed out by the UK government, the result was an immediate downgrade of its credit rating by Fitch's, one of the big three credit rating agencies whose role in creating the financial crisis was mentioned earlier (Guillam, 2011).

Beyond the UK, the success in Germany of medium-sized businesses with strong local roots and long-term ownership shows how it is perfectly possible for advanced industrial economies to sustain manufacturing firms and be perfectly profitable without becoming enmeshed in the snares of financial engineering. And in Denmark, business foundations support long-term development in high-tech sectors such as pharmaceuticals without exposing companies to the daily demands of the stock market (Jack, 2011). So there are alternatives to the new capitalism that has failed, and they can exist in the 'old economies' of Europe. This matters because although the free-market ideologues want to present us with the idea of an inexorable Asian rise and European decline, the reality is much less clear. As mentioned earlier, countries like the UK, Ireland, Spain and Iceland made a more or less full-on investment in the new capitalism and have been blown apart. Countries like Germany[6], Denmark, Sweden and Norway made much less investment in such ideas and seem to have more promising economic futures.

So organization studies has a part to play in diagnosing the organizational causes and consequences of the crisis of the new capitalism. But it also has an urgent agenda to identify new organizational models in response, to rediscover older but now abandoned organizational ideas, and to re-commit to those ways of organizing which, whilst abjured by new capitalism, have persisted.

the strange fates of management

There is an obvious but very far from trivial sense in which, given the high unemployment caused by the economic crisis, the concrete power of managers in the workplace has increased. The managerial right to manage is always stronger when the threat of dismissal is most frightening. And the fact that new capitalism also saw the erosion of trade union rights makes individual vulnerability to managerial power all the stronger. Beyond this, though, the place of management within the new capitalism is complex and contradictory. As I argued in Chapter 2, the high status of management was constructed over a long historical period as something necessary and valuable, to the point where it could be described by Peter Drucker in the mid-1950s as a bulwark of Western civilization. Sixty years on, that looks an almost absurd proposition. Instead, even managerially inclined writers could claim that 'there is a strong case that management ... could finally die out early in the twenty-first century' (Koch and Godden, 1996: 1). That prediction might well come true if the recent prescription of influential management guru Gary Hamel to 'fire all the managers' is followed (Hamel, 2011).

Even if we are sceptical of such pronouncements it seems clear that the employment prospects and working conditions of, especially, middle managers have been eroded. I have already suggested in Chapters 3 and 4 that this is so as a consequence of the increasing accent upon self-management. There is ample evidence that middle management has been under attack, illustrated by the demotic utterances of the 'guru' Tom Peters: 'Middle management ... is dead ... It's over, d'ya hear? Over. Over. Over' (cited in Thomas and Dunkerley, 1999: 157). I think we can interpret this to mean that Tom Peters thinks that middle management is over. It is tempting to dismiss such hyperbole, and it bears saying that claims about the imminent demise of management have been made for a very long time (e.g. Fletcher, 1973), but there is now a mass of well-researched studies attesting to the same thing (e.g. Wheatley, 1992; Heckscher, 1995; Thomas and Dunkerley, 1999; Kodz et al., 2003). This has led to the emergence of a white-collar 'underclass' whose travails in the USA are documented by Ehrenreich (2006). These are the laid-off middle managers consigned to increasing poverty and despair by the disjuncture between their former wealth, status and security and their redundancy, both literal and metaphoric, in new capitalism. Management may not have disappeared but, at the very least, the shine has gone off it as compared to its heyday in the post-war era.

This is illuminated by a study that some colleagues and I conducted (Brocklehurst et al., 2009). It was initially concerned with the knowledge brought by senior managers into the classroom when undertaking an Executive MBA programme. In the course of conducting interviews with these managers, we noticed that *not one* used the term 'manager' to describe themselves. So we conducted a follow-up study with a smaller number of them, drawn from different kinds of organizations and sectors, and asked about this. They told us that they did indeed abjure the term 'manager' for two broad reasons. First, they saw it as an over-used term in that it no longer denoted a person of any great seniority but was routinely used for quite low-level supervisory jobs. This is not quite to posit the 'end of management', but rather to say that it has spread to the point where it becomes meaningless. Second, and more importantly, they saw 'manager' as having a pejorative meaning of someone who was inflexible, unproductive and – horror of horrors – bureaucratic.

Clearly this links with the widespread demonization of bureaucracy discussed in Chapter 4, and by the same token the terms which these 'managers' preferred to use to describe themselves were part of the new lexicon of organizations. These terms included 'leader', 'entrepreneur', 'change agent' and 'consultant'. Of course Executive MBA students are a very particular group of managers, but this makes my point in that what their particularity consists of is that they are ambitious high-flyers who have a degree of choice as to how to describe themselves: and they choose not to describe themselves as managers.

The significance of this can be linked back to the three broad explanations of the *rise* of management that I reviewed in Chapter 2. To reprise, these were that management arose because of its technical advantages of co-ordination; because it delivered control of workers; and as a result of the manoeuvrings of an elite group. What can now be suggested is that all of these reasons for management have been eroded. The increasing tendency to subcontract and to buy in expertise on a temporary basis suggests a shift from hierarchical to market-based co-ordination; the increasing accent on self-management at least potentially obviates the need to external management of labour. But perhaps most important – given that, as we have seen, the extent of these new organizational practices is debatable – is the way that management has failed to perpetuate its elite status.

At the heart of that failure, I think, are the consequences of the new capitalism raised in this chapter. The original managerial revolution thesis, propounded most famously by James Burnham (1945), was, in summary, that:

> ... the largest corporations are now more often than not controlled by managers not owners ... managerial incentive systems are more closely tied to criteria other than company profitability ... [and] as a result ... most large firms are now oriented towards objectives beyond strict profit-maximization. (Useem, 1984: 29)

This, allied to the development of a technocratic welfare and military state during the Cold War period, accounts for Drucker's belief in the pivotal place of management in Western civilization. But as Sennett (2006) explains, this model of 'social capitalism' (as compared with 'new capitalism') has come apart not least as a result of the way that investors now have far more power in relation to the managers of corporations than they did in the mid-twentieth century. As financial markets were deregulated, massive flows of capital began to search out investment opportunities:

> Initially managers thought they were dealing with investors familiar to them from the past, that is, largely passive institutions and individuals. The workings of a firm would be confirmed at annual meetings where the only challenges would come from oddly dressed elderly ladies or vegetarian activists. The managers were soon disabused. Investors became active judges; a turning point ... occurred when pension funds, controlling vast quantities of capital, began actively pressuring management. The increasing sophistication of financial instruments like the leveraged buyout meant that investors could make or break corporations while its management stood helplessly by. (Sennett, 2006: 39)

In these conditions, industrial managers gave way to financiers who became, in the novelist Tom Wolfe's now famous, or infamous, phrase, the self-styled 'masters of the universe' (Wolfe, 1988). It was and is not enough for the management of a company to turn a profit: they are constantly pressurized to increase that profit under threat of a new management team being brought in. Moreover, the time frame within which profits and profit increases were required became shorter and shorter, and the speed with which trading could occur became faster and faster. In short, the capacity of management to pursue interests that diverged from profit-maximization has become significantly reduced, and with it the basis upon which it could be sustained as an elite. This is very evident in de Gaulejac's (2005: 9–12) poignant account of middle managers torn between their moral impulses to treat staff fairly and humanely and the over-weaning demands of market imperatives to do the opposite.

There is, however, a very significant contradiction in this. For whilst it is true that middle managers have declined in status and whilst it is true that the power of investors increased in the new capitalism, it is also the case that the very top managers have both retained and extended their power and privilege. Froud et al. (2006) argue convincingly, and in detail, that the financialization of business around shareholder value actually benefitted managers more than shareholders, as the former gained substantial pay increases. This is evident in the findings of the UK High Pay Commission (2011a) referred to earlier, showing how the pay of senior executives has hugely increased in recent decades. But it is most dramatically evident now that it has become clear that some of these top executives in the banking industry were taking decisions which, far from being to the benefit of their shareholders, actually led to the destruction of their organizations and massive losses to those shareholders.

This is very important because the standard defence of the pay levels of top managers in the new capitalism is that they reflect the value they added to their companies. But destroying those companies can hardly be seen as adding value, and in any case it is not just the cases of complete organizational collapse which are relevant here. The High Pay Commission found that top pay across business sectors was not linked to performance:

> there is rarely a link between directors' incentives and the way a company performs. In the past 10 years, the average annual bonus for FTSE 350 directors went up by 187 per cent and the average year-end share price declined by 71 per cent. (High Pay Commission, 2011b: 4)

This is not just about salaries but other benefits, including pensions. In the UK, as in many other countries, the pensions of rank and file employees of both private and public sectors are being cut back as they are deemed 'unaffordable'. Yet no such strictures apply to senior managers. For example, although the privatized, albeit heavily state-subsidized, railways in the UK are widely criticized for their performance and fare increases, their senior managers need not fear for their old age. Thus the outgoing chief executive of FirstGroup could reportedly look forward to a pension of £325,000 a year, even leaving aside millions of pounds worth of shares in the company (Lea, 2011). A little less than Fred Goodwin receives following the collapse of the Royal Bank of Scotland, admittedly, but it should still be possible to avoid having to take a part-time job in a supermarket to make ends meet. Even senior managers who make major mistakes do not suffer greatly. Forget the banks for a moment. In 2010 the finance director of TUI Travel, a large tour operator, was forced to resign after a £117m accounting error but weeks later reportedly received a payout of £757,000 (Pagnamenta, 2011).

So in these ways it seems fair to say that the new capitalism has gone hand in hand with the maintenance and enhancement of exactly the kind of managerial elite envisaged by Burnham. The difference compared with the 1950s and 1960s is that the elite has shrunk so as to encompass only the most senior managers alongside senior investment bankers, accountants, lawyers and so on. And whilst this top managerial elite may be most obvious in the private sector, it also exists, albeit to a lesser extent, in the public sector and for a very particular reason: the neo-liberal understandings of the superiority of private over public, and of human motivation being based on self-interest led to the idea that the only way to attract 'top managerial talent' to reform the public sector was to pay equivalent salaries to the private sector. Ironically, those same ideologues now point to the high pay of senior public sector managers as indicative of the wasteful bureaucracy of the state!

Beyond all of this, whatever the fate of *managers* there has been no demise in the power of *managerialism* (de Gaulejac, 2005; Locke and Spender, 2011). That is to say, the insinuation of a managerial, instrumentally rational, way of apprehending the world at large – work organizations included – continues unabated. Within organizations, we see a proliferation of attempts to measure and manage performance and the relentless attention to strategies, values, mission, quality, reorganization and so on discussed in previous chapters. Outside the workplace, as Hancock and Tyler (2008) show, more and more of everyday life is seen as being amenable to management. It now, perhaps, becomes clearer why in Chapter 2 I was at such pains to distinguish between management and managers. For whatever may be happening to the latter, management in the sense of a managerial way of looking at the world is in robust and swaggering form. Indeed, it is an irony that even as the flaws of the new capitalist model become apparent, the idea that it should be adopted within the public sector grows ever stronger as the financial engineers, having exhausted the gains from destroying the social capitalist settlement of the post-war era, greedily eye the profits they could make from the state sector, which is the last vestige of that settlement. Hence the nostrums of privatization and contracting-out of the public sector are, certainly within the UK, being applied ever-more extensively – some local councils, for example, are currently outsourcing their *entire* operations – as the neo-liberal zombie refuses to die (Crouch, 2011). Indeed, it would seem that the financial and economic crisis is the latest application of what Naomi Klein (2008) calls the 'shock doctrine' in which disaster is used as a cover for the imposition of, precisely, the doctrines of neo-liberalism and the new capitalism.

conclusion

I hope that it is obvious that what I have called here 'the new capitalism' constitutes far more than 'the environment' within which organizations operate or have operated. Indeed, as I suggested in Chapter 4, the idea of a hard and fast distinction of organization and environment is flawed anyway. As regards the new capitalism, organizations are both its medium and its outcome, the one is inseparably part and parcel of the other. Things like deregulation, privatization, managerialization, outsourcing, merging, acquiring, offshoring and financial engineering are things which organizations do, as well as have done to them. So, to make the point yet again, we cannot hope to study organizations properly without studying economics, politics and culture (and conversely, we cannot study those latter things properly without studying organizations). Of course to do so would require far more detailed analysis than I have provided here but, even so, I hope that the rough contours of new capitalism are clear.

It's important to re-state that the new capitalism did not represent a new epoch, and claims that it does are dangerous because they easily slide into the idea that it is something inevitable, a matter of the inexorable sweep of history rather than a determinate matter of the social and political choices we have made and are making. Rather, it is consistent with what relatively unregulated capitalism has always been. Indeed, what is beginning to be clear is that the period of social capitalism – that is, a regulated capitalism linked to welfarism – was particular to the four or five decades after the Great Depression and the Second World War. Nor are speculative booms new. Nevertheless, the consequences of new capitalism for organizations have been real and, in my view, deleterious. The economy of signs and space identified by Lash and Urry (1994) entails what is called 'deracination' – in other words, the destruction of roots. When there is little connection between places and communities on the one hand and production and consumption on the other, then the result is a certain kind of suffering (Bourdieu, 1999) and loss of social connection (Putnam, 2000). So, even when the new capitalism appeared to be working, there were many who questioned where it was leading us.

It seems almost quaint to recall it now, but some of those concerns were about the damaging effects of affluence (e.g. Layard, 2005; James, 2007; Naish, 2008) and especially the pace of life (e.g. Honoré, 2004).

These remain important issues both because they remind us of the false promise of new capitalism and because they act as a counter to any idea we should try to return to the days before the financial and economic crisis. But in any case, all of these criticisms, important as they are, have now been overtaken by that crisis, and any sufferings entailed by excessive affluence are now matched and exceeded by the real economic hardship and insecurity that have come in its wake. The scale of what is happening marks this out as being more than a fleeting economic downturn. Rather, 'assumptions that have prevailed since the 1980s embrace of the market lie in shreds'. Who said that? Some street-corner seller of the *Socialist Worker*? Well, no, it was Martin Wolf, Associate Editor of the *Financial Times* (Wolf, 2009). This, at least potentially, opens up the space for articulating new possibilities. The most important issue is to re-pose the question of what the purpose of human collective – i.e. organizational – activity is and whether current social and economic arrangements deliver it. This would be to open up the fundamental question of social philosophy: what is the good life and how is it to be achieved?

We should not seek to answer this question in terms of a return to some previous golden age. Not only is such time-travel impossible, it would also be undesirable: any supposed golden age inevitably, on closer examination, proves flawed. Nor need we answer this question in binary terms of capitalism or communism, and indeed few would now do so. It is quite possible to envisage systems that retain private property and market exchange – and are in this fundamental sense capitalist – but which are based upon local economies and work practices which are supportive of, rather than damaging to, human potentials and the environment (indeed to some extent this can be seen in the Scandinavian countries). Despite the stress in recent decades upon shareholder value and minimally regulated markets as unquestionably desirable, the historical truth is that capitalism has been at its most successful when regulated towards the consideration of wider concerns about social well-being and economic equality (and again the Scandinavian countries may be the best example of this). If new capitalism has indeed been deleterious to that well-being – both in terms of production and consumption – as has been suggested in this chapter, then that begins to make out the need for alternatives.

One of my favourite writers is the philosopher and theologian Simone Weil. She had much of interest to say about work and organizations, as

I have noted elsewhere (Grey, 1996). Amongst her works is a book called *The Need for Roots* (Weil, 1949). It is a difficult and complex book, as much spiritual as social scientific, and informed by her own time as a factory worker. She says that we need order, responsibility, hierarchy and honour if we are to live well. She did not mean the 'order' of the call centre script; not the 'responsibility' of the empowered employee; not the 'hierarchy' of the petty bureaucrat; not the 'honour' of the Masonic lodge. Rather, Weil expounds the dignity which comes from settled, meaningful work within settled, comprehensible communities. It is precisely the opposite of the endless deracination enacted by the new capitalism. There are better ways to organize than one which requires more and more work and more and more debt to buy more and more things when neither the work nor the things make us happy, and the debt is profoundly destabilizing. The apologists for new capitalism – and despite all that has happened, they still exist – insist that that which opposes them is some kind of old-fashioned elitism, but my objection to their world view is emancipatory rather than conservative: they are wedded to the inevitability of the future, no matter what the consequences, whereas I think we have choices. That we have not, thus far, exercised those choices as wisely as we might need not mean that we are debarred from doing so in the future. We should not, and cannot, separate the study of organizations from these choices.

notes

1 It is in the nature of what is being described that some of these examples may now have changed ownership.

2 And because of the sovereign debt crisis which I am about to discuss, there is little prospect of further state bailouts of failed banks in the way that happened in 2008. Bluntly, they do not have the resources to do this again, and at the time of writing it is not clear whether international bodies like the EU do either.

3 It is true that Bombardier subsequently (December 2011) won a £190m order (including a £80m state subsidy), but this was clearly on a very different scale to the order they failed to secure earlier.

4 It could rightly be said that the position of those within Western democracies remains considerably more privileged and secure than that of most of those in other parts of the world. But, apart from the fact that this book is addressed to its most likely readers in those Western countries, the key point is that the growing insecurity of

the West falsifies the claims made by the proponents of the new capitalism. They insisted that wealth would 'trickle down' so that the poorest in the world would be raised to the levels of the West. In fact what is happening is that the majority of those in the West are being made poorer.

5   Tax evasion means finding illegal ways not to pay tax unlike tax avoidance which finds legal ways to reduce tax liability.

6   It is true that Germany, as mentioned earlier, has significant banking exposure, and also that its potential role as a guarantor of Eurozone debts casts some shadows over its economic prospects. But levels of personal, corporate and state indebtedness are relatively low and it is a significant industrial exporter.

Conclusion:
Why Should Studying
Organizations Matter
to You?

Necessity is the plea for every infringement of human freedom.
It is the argument of tyrants and the creed of slaves.

William Pitt

Organizations matter because just about everything that we do occurs within an organization. The hospital where most of us are born, our playgroup, the doctor's surgery where we have our jabs, the infant, junior and secondary schools we attend, our university, our workplace, the government agencies which replace our hips and pay our pensions, the supermarkets where we shop, the banks and insurance companies we deal with, the travel agents and hotels which arrange our holidays, the media companies which provide our entertainment, the factories which make our cars and the garages which service them and provide their fuel, the coaches, trains and planes we use, the police and the army, the priest who buries us and the undertaker who digs our grave and provides the coffin: these are all organizational issues. How could organizations possibly not matter? We can all agree on that.

But this book has been concerned with a slightly different issue. Not organizations, as such, but *studying* organizations. This opens up the question of how we are to make sense of organizations. What concepts, ideas, theories, models and values are to be used not just to explain them but, often, to justify them or recommend their reform? This is the domain of organization theory. Now, for some, there may seem little difference between 'organizations' and 'studying organizations'. In the Introduction, I opened up the distinction between positivist and interpretivist or constructionist approaches to organization theory. For the positivists the relationship between organizations and studying organizations is, in principle, easy. All we need to do is to discover the facts of organizational life, no more and no less. In which case, why make life difficult for ourselves?

The problem, though, is that in organizations (and elsewhere in life) the facts do not speak for themselves. They are always interpreted and when the interpretations 'stick' and get believed by all or most people they become constructions. This issue can be seen even at the most basic level of defining what an organization is, as I discussed in Chapter 2 and again, in a different way, in Chapter 4.

Drawing the boundary is just that – drawing. We could include, say, pollution produced by a factory – or not; and this is not about facts but about interpretations. Does the factory end where its physical plant ends? Or does it end where the last molecule of its waste product is dispersed? Does it end when its workers sign off from their shift? Or does it end when the unemployed worker whose job has been 'off-shored' descends into depression and commits suicide? To those who confidently believe that the dividing line is self-evident I say: you mean that the interpretation of the dividing line is now so widely accepted as to be a construction.

If that argument is accepted then it follows that the construction (whatever it may be) is not *necessary*, in the sense of having to be that way, but contingent. It could be different. And for it to be different it must be reinterpreted. This is what gives the study of organization its importance, for it is crucially concerned with a contestation about what features of organizations will be noticed or ignored, emphasized or discounted, seen as important or dismissed as irrelevant. And to go back to my remarks in the Introduction about theory and practice, these interpretations are not just words or some separate domain from reality but are what determine what actually happens to people in the organizations which, we have agreed as common ground, are vitally important to everyone's lives.

For the bulk of mainstream organization theory, the interpretation and construction of organizations is almost always refracted through the lens of efficiency. This feeds through into a whole host of other constructions with which this book has been concerned, but it is the stress on efficiency which is central. In this respect, organization theory owes much to economics but, again as I said in the Introduction, what I want to urge is a political rather than an economic understanding of organizations. For the focus on efficiency creates some insuperable problems. One, important, way of thinking about this goes right back to Max Weber's work with which I began in Chapter 1. Weber's analysis of instrumental and substantive rationality marked a fault line in organization theory as well as being the originator of it as a 'subject'. The mainstream took instrumental rationality (or, for present purposes, efficiency) as being all that mattered; more critical approaches, such as mine, suggest that a focus on substantive rationality (for present purposes, politics, values and ethics) is the important issue.

From this perspective, the key question becomes: efficiency for whom? Traditional studies of organization only consider efficiency from the partial viewpoint of those who have an interest in a particular kind of efficiency. Normally this means the powerful – the people who own and run businesses being the obvious example. As soon as we shift position, efficiency can look quite different. Think of the now common way that all kinds of organizations use automated telephone systems, which I discussed in Chapter 4 in relation to customer focus. When we phone up we are told to press different keys for different options and eventually, probably after waiting in a queue, we are connected to a call centre, perhaps located halfway around the world to save labour costs. Now this is efficient for the organization as it is a low-cost way of managing enquiries, partly because some of the work formerly done by an employee is now done, for nothing, by the caller. Sometimes, as with computer support lines, for example, the caller actually pays whilst they do this unpaid work for the organization. So from the caller's point of view it is not efficient because it involves a waste of time, sometimes a cost and, often, frustration. Or, to take a different kind of example, related to what was talked about in Chapter 5, the business models of companies like Enron, Northern Rock, Royal Bank of Scotland and Lehman Brothers were all at one time hailed as efficient, and they certainly made some people very rich indeed. But in the light of the collapse of such companies and the effects on the world of their collapse, for whom were they efficient?

I suggest that mainstream approaches to studying organizations have embodied a one-sided answer to questions of efficiency which is predominantly concerned with management.[1] That is, the managerial interpretation of organizations has become constructed as if it were an objective reality, so that we typically forget its constructed nature. It is a necessity – the way things have to be – rather than a contingency. This entire book has been concerned to offer an interpretation of organization theory which tries to unravel the partiality and assumptions of the orthodox approach.

As soon as we start to question what seem like self-evident ideas about organizations, then a much more complex picture emerges. This picture just won't allow us to talk in vague terms about efficiency and getting the job done as if these terms absolve us from ethical and political choices. By 'ethical' I don't mean anything very philosophical, just judgements about what is right and wrong. By 'political' I don't mean the politics of politicians and governments, or at least not exclusively so.

I mean a wider sense of politics including the many ways that power is distributed and exercised, and the perpetual debates about, at the most general level, what to do and how to do it. My experience of management students, the most likely readers of this book, is that they often (but by no means always) hate this kind of talk. They don't want to think that managing organizations is about ethics and politics but would prefer to see it as about techniques, maybe even science, and regard any departure from this as an irrelevant waste of time. Well, sorry, but if you think this then you are wrong. What we do organizationally, including studying them, is always about ethics and politics. And, in a way, this is precisely because of the point with which I began this chapter. If so much of human life is organized, how could it be anything other than ethically and politically important? How could organizations inhabit some 'other world', separate from everything else? And isn't it ironic that those who adhere to such a view say that it describes the 'real world'?

I had a discussion with a student once which has always stuck in my mind. We were talking about scientific management. I was trying to say that efficiency might mean different things to different people. He nodded his head but then told me that this was 'just semantics' since what was *really* meant by efficiency was making the company more money. I asked him whether (in the context of Taylorism) it would seem to be 'just semantics' to be made to work harder or longer. My student didn't have an answer to that, but I could tell that he didn't really understand what I was asking, or thought it was irrelevant. For him, it was obvious that making 'the company' more 'efficient' was plain reality and everything else was 'just semantics' (I guess he would have expressed it less politely behind my back).

One way of understanding conventional organization theory is that it proposes a particular set of answers to ethical and political dilemmas so that, for my student, these dilemmas just don't exist. For a focus on efficiency from the point of view of the powerful (I will discuss in detail later what I mean by this word), and on organization and management as technique, *is* such an answer. In its extreme form, it is an answer which says that the interests of the powerful are paramount, and that anything that they want to do, and can do, is fair enough (ethically, that would be to say something like 'might is right'). I disagree fundamentally with this, or more mild versions of the same argument (for example, to take a common variant, that the powerful can do whatever they like so long as it is legal). I am certainly not alone in that disagreement but, it might be fairly said, so what? I'm free to disagree, so why go on about it?

I think there are good reasons why these arguments need to be made. First, there is the matter of general social responsibility. As I discussed

in Chapter 1, extreme versions of this one-sided rationality of organizations lead to truly horrific consequences, with the Nazi Holocaust
standing as the most awful example. Even if such situations don't currently seem to threaten, it is important always to remember that they
can come into existence if we are not vigilant. Of course there were
many reasons for Nazism and the Holocaust, most of which have little
to do with organization theory. But the techniques of organization and,
in particular, the blind pursuit of efficiency without regard to ethics
were certainly two of the things which enabled the Holocaust and,
more diffusely, the totalitarian management of the population at large.
If we subscribe to the precepts of technique and efficiency and nothing else,
then at the very least we have no defence against such events. I know that
people sometimes think that invocations of Nazism and the Holocaust are
overdone or inappropriate, and to some extent I agree, but it is important
to recognize how these and other horrors define the ultimate limit of what
is at stake when we discuss politics and ethics, and it would be more
crass to ignore them than to address them.

Moreover, even though we in the west may not currently seem to be
in danger of totalitarian politics and genocide, that does not mean
that organizations are not implicated within the production of same
fairly major forms of suffering. For example, we may when studying
organizations use the neutral sounding language of outsourcing and
human resource management but this can conceal some often appalling practices. Consider this:

> In Honduras, when filling out a particularly large order on a tight
> deadline, factory managers have been reported injecting workers with
> amphetamines to keep them going on forty-eight-hour marathons.
> (Klein, 2000: 216)

This story might be regarded as a one-off anomaly of no particular
interest, were it not for the fact that it fits a pattern of abuse for which
Klein, and many others, have provided considerable evidence. For
example, the International Labour Organization has identified the existence of some 850 'export processing zones' in which some 27 million
people work (cited in Klein, 2000: 215). And it is not just here where
people are organized in degrading ways. For example, it was not in the
developing world but in California, one of the richest places in the
world, where factory workers were forbidden to use the toilet but
instead told to urinate in their clothes, so that no production time was
lost (Perelman, 2005: 66–7). Such degradations seem far removed from
the airy atriums of business schools where 'efficient management practices'
are taught or the shiny corporate headquarters where they are practised,

but this doesn't undermine the complicity of those institutions in the suffering which they create and support. And it is no good saying that these examples belong somehow to an outdated world of early industrialism. They do not. They belong to the present day and if they are sometimes geographically remote that is only because of the globalization that is blithely mentioned as part of the 'context' of modern management.

Often closer to home, as shown in Chapters 3 and 4, there are techniques of organizational control in the form of culture management and its derivatives which exert an insidious influence on people in organizations, attempting to manipulate their very sense of self. Perhaps these are not so alarming as the sweatshops; perhaps they are more so. It really depends on whether you would prefer to be coerced into doing something knowing it is coercion, or manipulated into something not realizing that it is manipulation. I'm not sure what the answer to this is, but neither seems particularly appealing. Then again, in Chapter 5 I tried to depict the world of the new capitalist organizations animated more by short-term financial engineering than the long-term process of meeting human needs, and associated with an economy based upon unsustainable debt and which led to the major financial and economic crisis we are currently living through. Of course some readers will disagree with the way that I described that world, and I can accept that. But what it not acceptable would be to say that consideration of the world which organizations create and are created by is irrelevant to the study of organizations: not only is it relevant but it is central to what the entire purpose of such a study should be.

Second, beyond our general social responsibilities, these issues are particularly important to raise in the context of organization theory and management. A moment ago I said that conventional treatments of this subject could be seen as offering one kind of answer to political and moral issues, albeit one with which I disagreed. But it provides this answer in a very particular, and in my view entirely inadequate, way. It does it by pretending that the question does not exist. In other words, the assumptions about power, its distribution and its uses are presented as self-evident so that management is simply about technique.

One of the central ideas that informs the kind of work I do goes by the weighty name of 'de-naturalization' (Fournier and Grey, 2000). It means the attempt to expose and explain how those things which are taken to be natural or necessary – as 'just the way things are' and the way they need to be – are actually far from natural and are neither self-evident nor immutable. And this means that they never even get mentioned because why would anyone mention the patently obvious? But

I think that it is *precisely* these 'obvious' things which need to be thought about. It is striking that although we live, as discussed in Chapter 4, in an era when everything is seen as changeable and up for grabs that there are so many things which are just assumed without question to be immutable truths. Much of this book has been concerned with reinterpreting such supposed truths – about efficiency, 'personhood', choice, change and so on – in an attempt to show that they are contingent rather than necessary. If we realize that then new possibilities, not just for thought but for action, open up – for example in the ways that, as indicated in Chapter 5, the imperatives of the new capitalism can be questioned on grounds of the damage it has done to individuals and communities and societies, so as to open up the alternatives that might exist. Again, you may think that these alternatives are undesirable, but this does not mean that discussion of what are desirable ways to live can be avoided when studying organizations.

The assumptions about power that I have referred to are, precisely, assumptions, but they are embedded into organization theory and either not mentioned or mentioned only in a cursory way. One aspect of this is the way that organization theory is, or has become, so closely associated with management that, as I have been at pains to indicate in this book, to write about the one is almost to write about the other. The assumption here, which is absolutely an assumption about power, is that organization must mean hierarchy and a division of labour between 'managers' and others, whether they be called workers, professionals, employees, team members or even partners. So one – very specific – form of organizing becomes 'naturalized' as if it were synonymous with organization. Yet management is very far from being a natural or inevitable feature of organizations, either in general terms or in the specific forms it takes.

There are many other such assumptions built into conventional organization theory, revolving around all the issues of efficiency, rationality, power and so on which I have tried to problematize in this book. It is these that, taken together, constitute the ethical and political issues which I am saying should be central to studying organizations. And when I say central, this means that it is not enough to treat these, as often now happens on management courses (although even this is belated and often begrudged), as 'optional extras' along the lines of business ethics or corporate governance and social responsibility. For one thing, such 'optional courses' are usually unwilling to probe the very fundamental ethical and political issues which I have argued are important. But perhaps more importantly, and certainly relatedly, they fail to see how these fundamental issues are woven into the very fabric of organization theory and management.

To take an example which may clarify what I'm trying to get at, consider the issue of gender. Like business ethics, this has come somewhat on to the mainstream agenda of organizations, management and management education in recent years. Yet, like the bolt-on ethics courses, they typically take the form of 'women in management', and discussions of, for example, the 'glass ceilings' which act as obstacles to women gaining senior positions in organizations. Now this isn't entirely without merit, I would be the first to agree. But what it doesn't touch on is the fundamental issue that, as many feminist writers such as Kathy Ferguson (1984) have argued, organization and management (and the bodies of theory which relate to them) are inherently masculinist. That is, the preoccupation with order, control, instrumental rationality, hierarchy and domination are attributes of, if not men, then masculinist apprehensions of how to be in the world. I have put this in very general terms – although as indicated in the previous chapter it has specific applications in terms of macho management in the banking sector – because what I am getting at is that, on this view, gender issues cannot be treated as secondary or additional in studying organizations but are absolutely centrally implicated. This exemplifies the wider[2] points I have made about the need to place ethics and politics at the centre of the study of organizations.

So, beyond whatever general responsibility there is for anyone to be attentive to the political and ethical issues embedded in organization, there is a particularly pressing reason why organization theory, organization theorists and students of organization theory should be so.

why 'why?' matters more than 'how?'

In this book I have tried to argue that organization theory should be concerned with much more than efficiency in the narrow sense. But I have also advanced what is perhaps a more radical argument. It is that not only does the focus on the primacy of efficiency ignore things which are more important, but that even within its own terms it fails.

If this is true – and in a moment I will try to explain again why I believe that it is – then it represents a pretty damning indictment. For it would mean not only that organization theory doesn't do what I have argued it should do, but also that it doesn't even do what *it* says it should do. And it would also provide an answer to someone who had followed my arguments so far about how mainstream organization theory gives one kind of response to ethical and political issues, but who also agreed with that response and so would be quite happy just to get on with the pursuit of instrumental rationality in the service of the powerful. For of course this hypothetical person would be assuming that, within its narrow parameters, organization theory 'works'.

Now I have contended that there are not, and there cannot be, reliable organizational techniques if by that we mean actions (by managers, or others) which, if performed, will lead to predictable outcomes and only to those outcomes. Maybe this seems like a high hurdle to set, but it is precisely what is promised by standard organization theory. If techniques don't produce predictable effects, then what would be the point of having them, since there would be no reason to think that following them would do what was wanted? And it must be the case that, if predictable outcomes are required, then this can be met if *only* those outcomes are produced. Otherwise, even if we had a technique which had *some* predictable outcomes, there would be no way of knowing whether the unpredicted outcomes were more detrimental (just from the narrow standpoint of efficiency) than the benefits of the predicted outcomes. I appreciate that this is convoluted, but it is important to establish exactly what we are talking about.

I have already indicated, at several points in this book, why such techniques do not exist. The core theoretical issues are those I talked about in Chapter 1: unintended consequences, agency and the impact of these upon predictability. In the natural sciences, for some and indeed many practical purposes, predictability is possible because we can design out unintended consequences and we are dealing with objects which don't have agency. In social things, including obviously organizations, this is not true because people do have some degree of agency, the variables surrounding their behaviour are too many and varied to be designed out, and so predictions will not be reliable. And, as again was mentioned in Chapter 1, a particular feature of this is that the very fact of making predictions will set up the possibility that people will act differently precisely because of the predictions that have been made about them.

And this is not just true of 'people management' (which as I hope I showed in Chapter 2 is integrally and irreducibly contained within all modern conceptions of management). Even if we look at the supposedly hard, scientific aspects of management we find that there is no very good science. Thus, despite literally billions of pounds and literally millions of hours spent by hugely intelligent people trying to devise systems to beat the average of stock market performance, there is no system which in the long run is superior to making investments based upon random purchases of holdings.[3]

It is worth reflecting on what this means. As I suggested in Chapter 2, the conceit of people management is to draw into the managerial arena every feature of social life, a conceit extended in culture and change

management to attempts to mould people into a managerially acceptable shape, as discussed in Chapters 3 and 4. This opens up the idea that
both the formal and informal organization could be managed. Yet what
does such an idea amount to? The answer is very curious. If the formal
organization is the overt, public, managed parts and the informal is the
covert and spontaneous parts, then what the broad extension of management means is that the informal organization is itself manageable – that
is, that the 'newly discovered' informal organization is *actually* subsum-
able into the formal.

This simultaneous separation and re-incorporation of the informal into
the manageable is central to the modernist project of control and its
contemporary extensions. By naming and charting the informal domain,
this project renders that domain manageable, and it has to, for otherwise
control is not achievable. My thesis is that the informal always runs away
from attempts to enclose it, for that is what informal organization means.
So for every attempt to corral the informal into a managerial ambit, some
new possibility opens up; extending control always simultaneously opens
up new resistances. In this sense management is a perennially failing
operation, for each new domain into which it insinuates itself creates a
new border beyond which it does not have purchase.

Thus scientific management attempted to destroy informal relations
but, when these proved recalcitrant, the human relations approach
opened up a way to manage rather than to destroy informality. But that
approach, depending as it did on configuring human beings as fixed
entities to be motivated, accommodated and worked around, itself
informed more recent attempts to shape and mould humanity through
organizational culture. And these created costly commitments to providing a stable world for the new humans (for example, jobs for life or
pensions), and so post-bureaucracy and its permanent flux of change
morphing into a new capitalist economy of permanent restructuring
tries for the benefits of shaping people without the costs of doing so
organizationally. That story could be told in many ways, and it isn't by
any means the simple progression that I have depicted here. But the
point is just that any attempt to managerialize – to define, compute and
control – creates at the very point of that attempt the conditions for its
own failure, so that the task of management is never done, and never
could be done.

One reading of what I have said is that human beings will always find
a way of subverting, of being outside of, the hand of management. I am
inclined to think that this is true but not perhaps quite in the way that
might be assumed. For to make such an assumption is to posit humanity
as something which is ultimately knowable – perhaps in terms of thinking that there is a human spirit that makes them always want to resist.

But this is not quite my view. In this book I have argued that any attempt to pin down what it is to be human is a contingent construction. The same is true of invocations of the human spirit. The point is not that I, or anyone, can know something about the nature of humans that means they subvert being managed but that there is an ultimate 'unknowability' which perpetually limits management and also perpetually escapes any final definition of what it means to be human.

How abstract and pointless all this will seem to the more hard-headed readers of this book. They are wrong. For the assumptions of the hard-headed are just as abstract, but are rarely stated. And if stated and explored they would reveal why management, and the organization theory that supports it, are so problematic. For their flaws explain why management continues in a blind circle of solution to problem to solution to problem. And there is no point in saying that, in that case, the pragmatic manager will have nothing to do with organization theory. As I said in the Introduction, any kind of organizational practice, such as managing, presupposes an organization theory. Choosing to hold and act upon an unexamined theory will not prevent the problems identified within an examined theory, it will just make the perpetual failures of organization and management even more inexplicable.

Those who have read so far may believe they have spotted an obvious flaw in my argument. Their analysis might run thus. Grey, poor sap, is hopelessly confused. On the one hand, he says that ignoring values and ethics in favour of efficiency can lead to the nightmare of the administrative 'perfection' of the Holocaust. On the other hand, he says that administrative perfection is impossible because of unintended consequences, agency and the ultimate unknowability of human beings and the ultimate uncontrollability of the informal organization. Which is it?

My answer is that it is both. When I say that organizations will always defy management control, I do not mean that they will totally do so. The death camps restricted massively the space for informal organization, unintended consequences and human possibility. Yet even there, these things persisted. Read Primo Levi's (1979) account of the way that some prisoners 'made out' ways of surviving or – perhaps even more noteworthy from the perspective of this book – the description of the Danish organization theorist Gunnar Hjelholt of his time in a Nazi concentration camp (Madsen and Willert, 1996). Even horrific attempts at manageability fail, but they are horrific for all that. Everyday attempts fail even more. So what I am saying is that conventional organization theory, with its emphasis on control and efficiency, leads at one extreme to horror and at the other extreme to failure. And these extremes are not just a matter of chance, but grow ineluctably out of the way that we habitually think about organizations and their management.

Now let me imagine a different kind of objection. What about a hospital, trying to save lives through medical care. Shouldn't this be run as efficiently as possible since any wasted resources will mean that some-one who otherwise could be treated will die or suffer? Well, I agree – how could I not? But in this kind of case the organization is, presumably, animated by a substantively rational purpose (saving lives) and consid-erations of efficiency are in support of this purpose. There is nothing wrong with efficiency as a means if the end itself is justifiable in some other way that we agree is good. Of course in many cases there may be a disagreement about whether the purpose is good. Fine, but let's talk about that rather than assuming that efficiency is good in itself.

In any case, even in the hospital example, the nature of the purpose does not in itself undercut the concerns I have raised about efficiency. Let me give two kinds of example. First, many recent reforms of the UK National Health Service have been concerned to improve efficiency. One way that this has been done is to reduce spare capacity in the system. This in turn has the effect that unusual peaks in demand, such as a major incident or a flu epidemic, swamp the system. My imaginary objection carried the implication that I would be heartless to decry efficiency in health care, but I could just as easily say that it is heartless to cause people to suffer in the name of efficiency. For the question still remains: efficient for whom? Is spare capacity inefficient from the point of view of the patient caught up in a demand peak? My second example is a much more extreme variant of a similar point. In 2004 a nurse in the UK was successfully prosecuted because she had encouraged the deaths of near-death patients on her ward, apparently as a way of freeing beds for those who needed them, and could benefit more from them. In other words even murder was re-cast as efficient resource use. Efficiency is always a negotiated and contestable concept, which depends on value judgements (for example, what is the relative importance of patients with quite near or very nearly terminal conditions?).

My quarrel with organization theory in the mainstream incarnation that is largely taught in management and business schools (and practised by managers and consultants) is that it doesn't give anything like enough attention, not just to these difficult and extreme cases but to the under-lying issues that affect all organizations all of the time. It consistently puts the cart before the horse by emphasizing the 'how' of organizations rather than the 'why'. And this can't be remedied by doing a little bit of 'why' after the 'how', because the 'how' always contains assumptions about the 'why'. That is, the thing which should be the core of organization theory – the reasons, purposes or substantive rationality of organizations – are, at best, the periphery; whilst the periphery of organization theory, the way they achieve these purposes or instrumental rationality, is almost always the core.

Now that observation brings us to what has been a lurking theme within this book. For it is not just the *content* of organization theory but also its *context*: specifically, this means business schools. These are the places where I, and most current-day organizational theorists, work and where you, in all likelihood, study. It is really impossible to understand the nature – and in my view deficiencies – of much organization theory without considering this context.

The apparent purpose of business schools, to make their students better managers, is flawed. There is no evidence that they do – that is to say, there is no evidence that a manager who has studied at a business school is by any measure, no matter how broad or how narrow you choose it to be, better at managing than one who has not. Indeed one of the most noteworthy features of the new capitalism and the financial crisis discussed in Chapter 5 is how many of the managers of the organizations which failed were MBA-trained – Enron being a very clear example, but the investment banks, hedge funds and the consultants who advised them were (and are) all heavy users of such graduates (see James, 2009; Currie et al., 2010; Locke and Spender, 2011). This is not because business schools are engaged in any deliberate dishonesty, it is because they are an institutional expression of the failure of mainstream organization theory. That is, they subscribe to the dream of control without giving attention to the limitations of control I have identified in this book. You may be tempted to argue that organization theory is but one of the subjects of a management degree. But as I said in Chapter 2, all of them – marketing, strategy, operations management, accounting and so on – are in different ways concerned with representing and intervening in organizations. Since these organizations are inhabited by people, it follows that all the management subjects entail some kind of organization theory even if it isn't mentioned. Indeed, the less it is mentioned the more indefensible it is likely to be.

Yet, although management degrees manifestly and necessarily fail to do what they claim, they are very popular. Why? Because actually they are not about training students in skills but in training them in orientation (see Grey, 2002 for a full development of this claim). Business schools are not, currently, separate from the organizational world in the way that, for example, a politics department is (somewhat) separate from the political realm or a criminology department from the underworld. They are part and parcel of it. Which means that when we question the tenets of the *subject*, we must also question the *institutions* within which that subject is taught. Conventional organization theory is the organization theory of business schools and it teaches students that managerial control is both possible and desirable. However, the less conventional approach to organization theory that I have gestured towards in this book tells us something different. It tells us about the complexity of organizations, a complexity that makes them infinitely interesting. That, remember, was one purpose of this book – to say something interesting. Maybe I haven't succeeded, but even so it doesn't undercut the fact that organizations are interesting. They are interesting because it is never possible to say the final word about them. Because, as human collectivities, they contain all that is and could be human. Because, by doing so, they always defy complete description and control (or, to return to Chapter 2, representation and intervention). And this, which makes them interesting, is precisely what must be ignored by conventional, managerial representations of organization. For those representations *require* that organizations be nothing other than describable and controllable. So they must perforce suppress all the complexities which they do, in fact, contain.

Those readers, the majority, who are studying management will, I think, know or at least sense that the stuff they learn is all about avoiding this complexity. It tries to contain reality into flow-charts, matrixes, four-by-four tables and so on. But those same readers will surely also know that their own experience – just like that of all the people who inhabit organizations – cannot be encapsulated in such banalities. All that is interesting escapes these codifications. Most courses on organization try to suppress these complexities – that is why they are boring. Recognize the complexities and, suddenly, organization theory becomes really interesting. Being interesting about the study of organizations is not in the end, then, about accessible presentation although that may help; it is more about providing in terms of an analysis that which speaks of and to the complexity of organizations.

So why do I work in a business school, if all these places do is peddle a perverted version of organization theory and organizational life? In my darker moments I do not have an answer to this question, but I suppose it is because of the possibility of making a difference. Business schools offer a particular, perhaps unique, place where intellectuals (and I suppose I have to consider myself one, of sorts) can interact with society. There is no *necessary* reason why they should not offer an alternative understanding of the organizational world, and I have argued many times that there is a case for them to do so (e.g. Grey, 2004). For me to withdraw from them would represent a reduction – very small, but not absolutely negligible – in the likelihood of this happening. So I hope that the kind of arguments I have provided in this book act as a counter to more conventional approaches. At the very least I hope they encourage readers to be less gullible about the constant breathless hero-worship of business leaders, to see beyond cases studies of currently successful companies, and to be more critical of the business models of the new capitalism.

but still, why should i care?

I don't think that anyone who needs an answer to this question will have read this far, but it is possible that someone may skip to this final passage of the book to try to see whether it has anything for them. Well, the answer to that question is not really to do with this book but to do with you, the person reading it. Ultimately, the way you respond to studying organizations depends upon two interrelated factors: the political and the personal.

At the political level the question is the extent to which you accept current arrangements or think that they should change. My argument has been that organization theory as it is mostly taught is geared towards the production of conformity and because organizations are enmeshed with society, politics and economics this means conformity in those spheres too. The imperatives of efficiency, competition, market relations and so on lead to the conclusion that organizations have, of necessity, to be the way they are. I think that this view is deeply unsatisfactory, not just because it occludes key questions (such as, efficiency for whom?) but because it makes the frankly absurd assumption that the way that organizations are organized is efficient for anyone except a tiny minority. It isn't that organization theory delivers some way of organizing which is morally 'bad' yet managerially 'good'. What I have argued is that organization theory *does* deliver legitimation or justification for managers but *doesn't* reliably deliver efficiency.

If that is right then we have to ask, what value should be put upon managerial legitimation? If you are a manager of a corporation then of course the answer is probably: quite a bit, thank you. But is that good enough? John Rawls (1972) in his magisterial *A Theory of Justice* proposes a very elegant way of assessing social arrangements, of which organizations are a prime example. In brief, he asks what arrangements would be agreed to by people behind a 'veil of ignorance'. This means: what would people agree to if they did not know their income, gender, race, place in the hierarchy, bodily ability and so on? In the wider social sense Rawls argues that people would not agree to arrangements that substantially disadvantaged any one group, given that they did not know what group they would belong to.[4] In the organizational context it means that we might be unwilling to give pre-eminence to managerial interests given that we cannot know (from behind the veil of ignorance) whether these interests will be our own.

Rawlsian concepts of justice allow us to decouple organizational relations from interests. Given that most management students will be actual or aspirant managers, this is helpful in establishing an approach to organization theory which is detached from managerial interests. The entire tenor of managerialist thought is to propose that what is good for one is good for all. Why should such a constricted set of ideas about organizations be taken as organization theory? Only because the powerful have found it useful to them to do so. Ignore the interests of the powerful, as the Rawlsian veil of ignorance allows us to do, and things look very different. I would be surprised if anyone, not knowing whether they would be one of 'them' or not, would be happy to agree to an organizational world in which, to go back to a passage I quoted in Chapter 3, 'the idea is to educate people without them knowing it. Have the religion and not know how they got it' (Kunda, 1992: 5). Or, to give an example from earlier in this chapter, not knowing if they would be such a worker, would agree to an organizational world in which workers have to urinate in their clothes rather than take toilet breaks (Perelman, 2005: 66–7). Or, more prosaically, not knowing where they were on the increasingly unequal income and wealth distribution scale discussed in Chapter 5, would agree to that as a fair distribution.

However, Rawls's formulation, although helpful in thinking about interests, does not go far enough. Despite my talk here and elsewhere in this book about 'the powerful', power is far more complex than such talk would suggest. We cannot see the world in terms of oppressors and victims or managers and workers because each of these is both implicated in, and produced through, power relations. An example, mentioned in Chapter 3, is the way that ludicrously hardworking managers and professionals are themselves fostered by organizational regimes that promote a sense of self-managed responsibility.

In this sense, my analysis of organization theory is different to the traditional left-wing complaint about the oppression and exploitation of workers, such as has been associated with traditional critiques from, in particular, labour process analysis (Braverman, 1974). For my belief is that organization theory subjugates almost all of us and, indeed, that the relatively petty differences between 'workers' and 'managers' lead to the latter being terrified to question the established order for fear of losing their small advantages. This is all the more true as many kinds of managerial employment become less secure, as discussed in Chapter 5.

I don't mean by this that I don't understand the difference in life experience between, say, a sweatshop worker in a shoe factory in the Philippines working almost incredibly long hours for a pittance, and a middle manager of a footwear conglomerate, living in a British commuter village, stressed out by the endless demands for cost savings and fearful of the next round of downsizing. In a real material sense, the former is much worse off than the latter. It's just that I see them as both locked within a common understanding of organizations, and locked within it whether they agitate for more from, or devise ways of giving less to, each other. Indeed, I think that only by recognizing their *interdependence* can any real progress be made. And that interdependence is masked by conventional organization theory because just as it makes the Philippino worker the object of the British manager's efficiency gain, it tries to make that manager embrace as a 'religion' the corporate imperatives of the organization that employs them both.

In Chapter 5 I tried to draw out the implications of all this by discussing the nature of the new capitalism – in which organizations are sites not primarily for delivering goods and services that people need but for a financial engineering which demands endless restructuring and more and more intense work, and is dependent upon a massive debt delivered via an inherently fragile financial system. The fundamental question we have to ask is: why? Who is this good for? It propels us into a world not only of ever-greater stress but also one which undermines social and communal bonds. It detaches organizations from places and people, and in return delivers an economic growth which does not make people happy – and perhaps makes people less happy – even when it sometimes makes them richer, and which is deleterious to the environment as well as to social well-being. It places us on a lifelong and ever-faster spinning hamster wheel of work, debt and consumption. And this is just what happens when the new capitalism is working as it is supposed to! But note yet again that the issue is not 'well it might have its problems but it works'. Because what the financial and economic crisis has shown very clearly is that the new capitalism and the organizational forms it created do not, even in a narrow functional sense, 'work'.

Ultimately, then, we have to take a stance on the politics of all this. But our capacity to do so is also about our personal or psychological commitments. These are not separate things. Traditional socialist takes on these issues assumed that the issues were objective. The oppressed worker in the Philippines or anywhere else would have a natural interest in challenging the power of the multinational, just as the financier in London or anywhere else would have a natural interest in supporting that power. Nonsense. The worker might well be dreaming of and working towards the day when she or he had saved up enough money to set up their own business, or for their child to do so, or – who knows – for their child to attend a business school to study organizations! The financier might well dream of having the courage to depart the 'rat race' and raise chickens on an organic smallholding. Although their experiences, choices and material prosperity are very different, both of these hypothetical people are linked in a systemic way.

The word 'systemic' is important, because it suggests that there is much more at stake here than the individual choices which people can (or cannot) make within the system in which they operate. And one part – minor for sure but not entirely insignificant – of that system is the institutions where organizations and management are studied. At the moment, I think that these institutions do a generally poor job of dealing with what is at stake in such study but, as with everything I have said in this book up to now, I do not think there is any necessity here. It seems to me perfectly possible that the manager or aspirant manager can take a non-managerialist view, and certainly that organizations can be about more than instrumental rationality. I would hardly have written this book if I did not believe this to be so and recent economic events may yet make it more likely to become so.

However, my experience is that, even now, far too many managers and management students (and, indeed, others) like the certainties of the conventional approach. Too many buy into macho management because more fundamentally they buy into the idea that caring about others is wimpy. Too many embrace selfishness because they have yet to experience profoundly, and ignore their daily experiences of, their dependence on others. Too many embrace certainty because they are terrified by its alternative. Too many lack imagination, empathy and insight into others, so it is small wonder they embrace the truncated, stunted and callous version of organization theory against which I have been arguing. However, it is surely also the case that many managers, students and others do not lack imagination, empathy and insight, and for them the issue is rather that the way in which they are encouraged to study organizations gives little or no space for them to understand how it can be wider, richer and more engaged.

Studying organizations is inseparable from political choices. In mainstream approaches, these choices are largely ignored when it is assumed that organizations are, and should be, no more than sites of instrumentally rational control. What a deficient and damaging view of life that is – almost as damaging to those who hold it as it is to everyone else. But aside from the deficiencies are the absurdities. For even within that narrow view what is abundantly clear is that organizations cannot be controlled that way. And what is at stake when we study organizations is not words on a page, but the way in which these relate to and inform actions that impact upon the world in terms of the way people are treated at work, the way that we provide for ourselves and others, and the consequences of this for the environment and for social well-being.

So that, finally, is the issue. The stakes are very high. What kind of world do you want? It has to be an organizational world for, so far as I can see, there is no other on offer. The choice is both political and personal. Politically, the world offered by conventional organization theory is hideously distorted by managerialism in the sense that it treats managerial concerns and realities as being identical with what is true of organizations in general. It ignores all the consequences of organizations except for those that figure in a narrow calculus of a one-sided notion of efficiency. Personally, the world offered by conventional organization theory appeals only to those willing to distort themselves and others in line with stunted notions of people as controlled and controlling at the expense of the true range of their human potentials. Truth is always elusive, but the manifest distortions entailed by both of these positions make it self-evident to me that they cannot be true. The purpose of this short book has been to say some things about the study of organizations which seem to me to be true.

▨▨▨ notes

1 To be sure, organization theory is only one aspect of this construction which fits into wider political and ideological constructs and contexts.
2 Wider in the sense that I have tried to problematize organization theory on a number of grounds, not just those relating to gender. Nevertheless, my arguments are, I think, often consistent with, and certainly informed by, feminist analysis.
3 What underlies this is that so-called 'management science' is *always* a version of 'people management'. The market is not an abstract entity but consists of a great many people moved by individual emotion, shared assumptions, group dynamics and even hysteria. Supposedly scientific models of these markets fail, not because they fail to recognize that it is people who inhabit financial markets but because they fail to recognize that these people can never be 'modelled'. Hence financial analysts always have recourse to cod psychology, e.g. market 'confidence'.
4 Astute readers will note that Rawls's theory of justice is, in effect, a restatement of the Kantian categorical imperative outlined in Chapter 1. However, the striking 'veil of ignorance' metaphor is a good way of operationalizing Kantian ethics.

Recommended Reading

Ten books I would recommend on the things discussed in this book:

Anthony, P. (1977) *The Ideology of Work*. London: Routledge.

Bauman, Z. (1989) *Modernity and the Holocaust*. Cambridge: Polity.

du Gay, P. (2000) *In Praise of Bureaucracy*. London: Sage.

Jacques, R. (1996) *Manufacturing the Employee*. London: Sage.

Lanchester, J. (2010) *Whoops! Why Everyone Owes Everyone and No One Can Pay*. London: Penguin

Locke, R. and Spender, J-C. (2011) *Confronting Managerialism: How the Business Elite and Their Schools Threw Our Lives Out of Balance*. London: Zed Books

Parker, M. (2002) *Against Management*. Cambridge: Polity.

Rose, N. (1989) *Governing the Soul*. London: Routledge.

Sennett, R. (2006) *The Culture of the New Capitalism*. New Haven, CT: Yale University Press.

Shenhav, Y. (1999) *Manufacturing Rationality*. Oxford: Oxford University Press.

References

Aldrich, H. (1979) *Organizations and Environments*. Englewood Cliffs, NJ: Prentice-Hall.

Alvesson, M. (ed.) (2011) *Classics in Critical Management Studies*. Cheltenham, UK: Edward Elgar.

Alvesson, M. and Willmott, H. (eds) (1992) *Critical Management Studies*. London: Sage.

Asia Development Bank Institute (2010) 'The role played by credit rating agencies in the financial crisis'. Available at http://www.adbi.org/working paper/2010/01/26/3446.credit.rating.agencies.european.banking/ the.role.played.by.credit.rating.agencies.in.the.financial.crisis. Accessed 21/12/11.

Aubenas, F. (2011) *The Night Cleaner*. Cambridge: Polity Press.

Balzli, B. (2010) 'How Goldman Sachs helped Greece to mask its true debt', *Spiegel Online*. Available at http://www.spiegel.de/international/ europe/0,1518,druck-676634,00.html. Accessed 14/12/11.

Baritz, S. (1960) *Servants of Power*. Middletown: Wesleyan University Press.

Basso, P. (2003) *Modern Times, Ancient Hours: Working Lives in the 21st Century*. London: Verso.

Bauman, Z. (1989) *Modernity and the Holocaust*. Cambridge: Polity.

BBC (2003) 'German cannibal tells of fantasy'. Available at http://news. bbc.co.uk/1/hi/3286721.stm. Accessed 27/12/11.

Berry, A., Capps, T., Cooper, D., Tinker, T. and Lowe, E. (1987) 'The ethics of research in a public enterprise', in F. Heller (ed.), *The Uses and Abuses of Social Science*. London: Sage. pp. 85–98.

Blackhurst, C. (2010) 'Cadbury takeover shows how bankers really make their money'. Available at http://www.thisislondon.co.uk/standard/ article-23797771-cadbury-takeover-shows-how-bankers-really-make-their-money.do. Accessed 30/12/11.

Blau, P. (1955) *The Dynamics of Bureaucracy*. Chicago: Chicago University Press.

Boles, N. (2010) *Which Way's Up? The Future for Coalition Britain and How to Get There*. London: Biteback.

Boltanski, L. and Chiapello, E. (2007) *The New Spirit of Capitalism*. London: Verso.

Bourdieu, P. (ed.) (1999) *The Weight of the World: Social Suffering in Contemporary Society*. Cambridge: Polity.

Braverman, H. (1974) *Labor and Monopoly Capital*. New York: Monthly Review Press.

Brocklehurst, M., Grey, C. and Sturdy, A. (2009) 'Management: The work that dares not speak its name', *Management Learning* 41 (1): 7–19.

Burnham, J. (1945) *The Managerial Revolution*. London: Penguin.

Burrell, G. (1988) 'Modernism, postmodernism and organizational analysis: the contribution of Michel Foucault', *Organization Studies* 9 (2): 221–35.

Business Insider (2011) 'Here's what Europe can learn from the Icelandic default model'. Available at http://www.businessinsider.com/iceland-default-2011-11. Accessed 15/12/11.

Cameron, D. (2010) 'From central power to people power'. Available at http://www.conservatives.com/News/Speeches/2010/02/David_Cameron_From_central_power_to_people_power.aspx. Accessed 10/12/11.

Carnall, C. (1995) *Managing Change in Organizations*. 2nd edn. London: Prentice-Hall.

Carnall, C. (2007) *Managing Change in Organizations*. 5th edn. London: Prentice-Hall.

Caulkin, S. (2007) 'How ICI settled on the wording of its epitaph', *Observer*. Available at http://www.guardian.co.uk/business/2007/jun/24/manufacturing.observerbusiness. Accessed 24/06/07.

Chakrabortty, A. (2011) 'The decline of Britain's train-manufacturing industry: Who is to blame', *Guardian Online*. Available at http://www.guardian.co.uk/commentisfree/2011/jul/11/decline-britains-train-manufacturing-industry. Accessed 11/07/11.

Chrisafis, A. (2003) 'Fiascos that haunt "can do" company', *Guardian Online*. Available at http://www.guardian.co.uk/environment/2003/feb/15/londonpolitics.congestioncharging. Accessed 10/12/08.

Costas, J. and Fleming, P. (2009) 'Beyond dis-identification: A discursive approach to self-alienation in contemporary organizations', *Human Relations* 62 (3): 353–78.

Crenson, M. (1971) *The Unpolitics of Air Pollution*. Baltimore, MD: Johns Hopkins Press.

Crosby, P. (1979) *Quality is Free*. New York: McGraw-Hill.

Crouch, C. (2011) *The Strange Non-Death of Neoliberalism*. Cambridge: Polity.

Crozier, M. (1964) *The Bureaucratic Phenomenon*. Chicago: University of Chicago Press.

Currie, G., Knights, D. and Starkey, K. (2010) 'Introduction: A post-crisis critical reflection on business schools', *British Journal of Management* 21 (supplementary issue): 1–5.

Daintith, J. (ed.) (2000) *Quotations for Speeches*. London: Bloomsbury.

Dalton, M. (1959) *Men who Manage*. New York: John Wiley & Sons.

Das, S. (2011) *Extreme Money. The Masters of the Universe and the Cult of Risk*. Harlow, UK: Pearson Education.

De Gaulejac, V. (2005) *La Société Malade de la Gestion: Idéologie Gestionnaire, Pouvoir Managerial at Harcèlement Social*. Paris: Éditions du Seuil.

Delbridge, R. (1998) *Life on the Line in Contemporary Manufacturing*. Oxford: Oxford University Press.

Department for Social Development (2011) 'The cost of benefit fraud'. Available at http://www.dsdni.gov.uk/the-cost-of-benefit-fraud. Accessed 12/12/11.

DiMaggio, P. and Powell, W. (1983) 'The iron cage revisited: Institutional isomorphism and collective rationality in organizations', *American Sociological Review* 48 (1): 147–60.

Drucker, P. (1955) *The Practice of Management*. London: Heinemann.

du Gay, P. (2000) *In Praise of Bureaucracy: Weber, Organization and Ethics*. London: Sage.

du Gay, P. (2003) 'The tyranny of the epochal: Change, epochalism and organizational reform', *Organization* 10 (4): 663–84.

Ehrenreich, B. (2006) *Bait and Switch: The Futile Pursuit of the Corporate Dream*. London: Granta.

Elliott, L. and Atkinson, D. (2007) *Fantasy Island*. London: Constable Robinson.

Engelen, E., Erturk, U., Froud, J., Johal, S., Leaver, A., Moran, M., Nilsson, A. and Williams, K. (2011) *After the Great Complacence: Financial Crisis and the Politics of Reform*. Oxford: Oxford University Press.

Fenton-O'Creevey, M., Nicholson, N., Soane, E. and Willman, P. (2005) *Traders, Risks, Decisions and Management in Financial Markets*. Oxford: Oxford University Press.

Ferguson, K. (1984) *The Feminist Case against Bureaucracy*. Philadelphia, PA: Temple University Press.

Fineman, S. (1996) 'Emotion and organizing', in S. Clegg, C. Hardy and W. Nord (eds), *The Handbook of Organization Studies*. London: Sage. pp. 543–64.

Fleming, P. (2005) 'Workers' playtime: Boundaries and cynicism in a "culture of fun" program', *Journal of Applied Behavioural Science* 41 (3): 285–303.

Fleming, P. and Spicer, A. (2004) 'You can check out anytime, but you can never leave: Spatial boundaries in a high commitment organization', *Human Relations* 57 (1): 75–94.

Fletcher, C. (1973) 'The end of management', in J. Child (ed.), *Man and Organization*. London: Allen & Unwin. pp. 135–57.

Folkman, P., Froud, J., Johal, S. and Williams, K. (2006) 'Working for themselves? Capital market intermediaries and present day capitalism', *Centre for Research on Socio-Cultural Change Working Paper 25*. Milton Keynes: Open University.

Foucault, M. (1979) *Discipline and Punish*. London: Penguin.

Foucault, M. (1991) 'Governmentality', in G. Burchell, C. Gordon and P. Miller (eds), *The Foucault Effect: Studies in Governmentality*. London: Harvester Wheatsheaf. pp. 87–104.

Fournier, V. and Grey, C. (2000) 'At the critical moment: Conditions and prospects for critical management studies', *Human Relations* 53 (1): 7–32.

Fromm, E. (1942) *Fear of Freedom*. London: Routledge & Kegan Paul.

Froud, J., Johal, S., Leaver, A. and Williams, K. (2006) *Financialization and Strategy: Narratives and Numbers*. London: Routledge.

Gee, J., Hull, C. and Lankshear, C. (1996) *The New Work Order: Behind the Language of the New Capitalism*. Sydney: Allen & Unwin.

Gewirtz, S. (2002) *The Managerial School*. London: Routledge.

Giddens, A. (1984) *The Constitution of Society*. Cambridge: Polity.

Gouldner, A. (1954) *Patterns of Industrial Bureaucracy*. New York: Free Press.

Grey, C. (1996) 'Towards a critique of managerialism: The contribution of Simone Weil', *Journal of Management Studies* 33 (5): 591–611.

Grey, C. (1999) 'We are all managers now, we always were: On the development and demise of management', *Journal of Management Studies* 36 (5): 561–86.

Grey, C. (2002) 'What are business schools for? On silence and voice in management education', *Journal of Management Education* 26 (5): 496–512.

Grey, C. (2003) 'The real world of Enron's auditors', *Organization* 10 (3): 572–6.

Grey, C. (2004) 'Reinventing business schools: The contribution of critical management education', *Academy of Management Learning and Education* 3 (2): 178–86.

Grey, C. (2010) 'Organizing studies: Publications, politics and polemic', *Organization Studies* 31 (6): 677–94.

Grey, C. and Sinclair, A. (2006) 'Writing differently', *Organization* 13 (3): 443–53.

Grey, C. and Willmott, H. (eds) (2005) *Critical Management Studies: A Reader*. Oxford: Oxford University Press.

Grint, K. (1997) *Fuzzy Management*. Oxford: Oxford University Press.

Guillam, P. (2011) 'Ratings agencies must not derail Co-operative bank'. Available at http://www.guardian.co.uk/commentisfree/2011/dec/20/ratings-agencies-co-operative-bank-lloyds. Accessed 20/12/11.

Gupta, P. (2005) *The Six Sigma Performance Handbook*. New York: McGraw-Hill.

Hacking, I. (1983) *Representing and Intervening*. Cambridge: Cambridge University Press.

Hacking, I. (1991) 'How should we do the history of statistics?', in G. Burchell, C. Gordon and P. Miller (eds), *The Foucault Effect: Studies in Governmentality*. London: Harvester Wheatsheaf. pp. 181–96.

Hamel, G. (2011) 'First, let's fire all the managers', *Harvard Business Review*, December.

Hammer, M. and Champy, J. (1993) *Reengineering the Corporation: A Manifesto for Business Revolution*. London: Nicholas Brealey.

Hancock, P. and Tyler, M. (eds) (2008) *The Management of Everyday Life*. Basingstoke: Palgrave.

Harding, N. (2003) *The Social Construction of Management*. London: Routledge.

Heckscher, C. (1994) 'Defining the post-bureaucratic type', in C. Heckscher and A. Donnellon (eds), *The Post-bureaucratic Organization: New Perspectives on Organizational Change*. Thousand Oaks, CA: Sage. pp. 14–62.

Heckscher, C. (1995) *White Collar Blues*. New York: Basic Books.

Heffernan, R. (2001) *New Labour and Thatcherism: Political Change in Britain*. Basingstoke, UK: Palgrave.

High Pay Commission (2011a) *Cheques Without Balances: Why Tackling High Pay is in the National Interest*. Available at http://high paycommission. co.uk/facts-and-figures/final-report-cheques-with-balances-why-tackling-high-pay-is-in-the-national-interest/. Accessed 14/12/11.

High Pay Commission (2011b) *What are We Paying For? Exploring Executive Pay and Performance*. Available at http://highpaycommission. co.uk/wp-content/uploads/2011/09/HPC-DPperformance.pdf. Accessed 18/12/11.

Hirst, P. and Thompson, G. (1996) *Globalization in Question*. Cambridge: Polity.

Honoré, C. (2004) *In Praise of Slow*. London: Orion.

Huxley, A. (2006/1932) *Brave New World*. New York: Harper Collins.

Jack, A. (2011) 'A model for healthier profits', *Financial Times*, 6 December, p. 16.

Jackson, B. and Parry, K. (2011) *A Very Short, Fairly Interesting and Reasonably Cheap Book about Studying Leadership*. 2nd edn. London: Sage.

Jacques, R. (1996) *Manufacturing the Employee: Management Knowledge from the 19th to the 21st Centuries*. Thousand Oaks, CA: Sage.

James, A. (2009) 'Academies of the apocalypse', *Guardian Online*. Available at http://www.guardian.co.uk/education/2009/apr/07/mba-business-schools-credit-crunch/print. Accessed 25/10/11.

James, O. (2007) *Affluenza*. London: Random House.

Kamata, S. (1982) *Japan in the Passing Lane: An Insider's Account of Life in a Japanese Auto Factory*. New York: Pantheon.

Kanter, R.M. (1977) *Men and Women of the Corporation*. New York: Basic Books.

Kelly, C. (2011) 'Broken chocolate factory pledge devastates Keynsham'. Available at http://www.bbc.co.uk/news/uk-england-bristol-12126550. Accessed 18/09/11.

Kenny, K., Whittle, A. and Willmott, H. (2011) *Understanding Identity and Organizations*. London: Sage.

Kettle, M. (2010) 'The credit rating agencies are leading an assault on nations and peoples', *Guardian Online*. Available at http://www.guardian.co.uk/commentisfree/2010/dec/16/credit-rating-agencies-downgrade-spain. Accessed 16/10/10.

Klein, N. (2000) *No Logo*. London: Flamingo.

Klein, N. (2008) *The Shock Doctrine: The Rise of Disaster Capitalism*. London: Penguin.

Knights, D. (1992) 'Changing spaces: The disruptive impact of a new epistemological location for the study of management', *Academy of Management Review* 17: 514–36.

Koch, R. and Godden, I. (1996) *Managing without Management: A Post-management Manifesto for Business Simplicity*. London: Nicholas Brealey.

Kodz, J., Davis, S., Lain, D., Strebler, M. and Rick, J. (2003) *Working Long Hours: A Review of the Evidence*. DTI Employment Relations Research Series, ERRS16. London: HMSO.

Kunda, G. (1992) *Engineering Culture*. Philadelphia, PA: Temple University Press.

Lanchester, J. (2010) *Why Everyone Owes Everyone and No One Can Pay*. London: Penguin.

Lash, S. and Urry, J. (1994) *Economies of Signs and Space*. London: Sage.

Layard, R. (2005) *Happiness: Lessons from a New Science*. London: Penguin.

Lea, R. (2011) 'The train now leaving is the pension express', *The Times*, 5 February, p. 35.

Levi, P. (1979) *If This is a Man/The Truce*. London: Penguin.

Lewin, C. (1951) *Field Theory in Social Science*. New York: Harper & Row.

Liker, J. and Hoseus, M. (2008) *Toyota Culture: The Heart and Soul of the Toyota Way*. New York: McGraw-Hill.

Locke, R. (1996) *The Collapse of the American Management Mystique*. Oxford: Oxford University Press.

Locke, R. and Spender, J-C. (2011) *Confronting Managerialism: How the Business Elite and Their Schools Threw Our Lives Out of Balance*. London: Zed Books.

Lukes, S. (1974) *Power: A Radical View*. London: Macmillan.

Luttwak, E. (1999) *Turbocapitalism: Winners and Losers in the Global Economy*. New York: Harper Collins.

MacIntyre, A. (1981) *After Virtue*. London: Duckworth.

Madsen, B. and Willert, S. (1996) *Survival in the Organization: Gunnar Hjelholt Looks Back at the Concentration Camp from an Organizational Perspective*. Aarhus, Denmark: Aarhus University Press.

Mant, A. (1977) *The Rise and Fall of the British Manager*. London: Macmillan.

March, J. (2000) 'Plenary Address', 16th EGOS Colloquium, Helsinki, Finland, July 2–4.

Meek, V. (1988) 'Organizational culture: Origins and weaknesses', *Organization Studies* 9 (4): 453–73.

Merkle, J. (1980) *Management and Ideology*. Berkley, CA: University of California Press.

Merton, R. (1940) 'Bureaucratic structure and personality', *Social Forces*, May: 560–8.

Murphy, R. (2011) *The Courageous State: Rethinking Economics, Society and the Role of Government*. London: Searching Finance.

Naish, J. (2008) *Enough: Breaking Free from the World of More*. London: Hodder & Stoughton.

National Audit Office (NAO) (2002) 'Individual Learning Accounts' (Press Notice 60/02). Available at http://www.nac.org.uk/pn/ø1-ø2/ø1ø21235.ntm. Accessed 13/06/08.

OECD (2011) *An Overview of Growing Inequalities in OECD Countries: Main Findings*. Available at http://www.oecd.org/dataoecd/40/12/49170449.pdf. Accessed 14/12/11.

Ogbonna, E. and Wilkinson, B. (1988) 'Corporate strategy and corporate culture: The view from the checkout', *Personnel Review* 19 (4): 9–15.

Orwell, G. (1946) 'James Burnham and the managerial revolution', *New English Weekly*, May. Available at http://www.k-1.com/Orwell/site/work/essays/burnham.html. Accessed 17/01/08.

Orwell, G. (1949) *Nineteen Eighty-four*. London: Secker & Warburg.

Pagnamenta, R. (2011) 'System failure and resignation are no bar to share of £4.9m payout', *The Times*, 3 January, p. 35

Parker, M. (2002) *Against Management*. Cambridge: Polity.

Parker, M., Fournier, V. and Reedy, P. (eds) (2007) *The Dictionary of Alternatives: Utopianism and Organization*. London: Zed Books.

Parker, M., Cheney, G., Fournier, V. and Land, C. (eds) (2013, forthcoming) *The Routledge Companion to Alternative Organizations*. London: Routledge.

Parker, S., Brown, R., Child, J. and Smith, M. (1977) *The Sociology of Industry*. London: Allen & Unwin.

Pascale, R. and Athos, A. (1982) *The Art of Japanese Management*. London: Penguin.

Perelman, M. (2005) *Manufacturing Discontent: The Trap of Individualism in Corporate Society*. London: Pluto.

Peters, T. and Waterman, R. (1982) *In Search of Excellence*. New York: Harper & Row.

Pettifor, A. (2006) *The Coming First World Debt Crisis*. Basingstoke, UK: Palgrave.

Putnam, R. (2000) *Bowling Alone*. New York: Simon & Schuster.

Rawls, J. (1972) *A Theory of Justice*. Oxford: Oxford University Press.

Reinhart, C. and Rogoff, K. (2009) *This Time is Different: Eight Centuries of Financial Folly*. Princeton, NJ: Princeton University Press.

Reiss, H. (ed.) (1991) *Kant: Political Writings*. Cambridge: Cambridge University Press.

Roberts, J. (1984) 'The moral character of management practice', *Journal of Management Studies* 21 (4): 287–302.

Roberts, J. and Armitage, J. (2006) 'From organization to hypermodern organization: The accelerated appearance and disappearance of Enron', *Journal of Organizational Change Management* 19 (5): 558–77.

Rose, N. (1989) *Governing the Soul*. London: Routledge.

Rosen, M. (1988) 'You asked for it: Christmas at the bosses' expense', *Journal of Management Studies* 25 (5): 463–80.

Schwartz, B. (2004) *The Paradox of Choice: Why More is Less*. New York: Harper Perennial.

Schwartzman, H.B. (1993) *Ethnography in Organizations*. Qualitative Research Methods Series No. 27. Newbury Park, CA: Sage.

Semler, R. (1993) *Maverick*. London: Century.

Sennett, R. (1998) *The Corrosion of Character: The Personal Consequences of Work in the New Capitalism*. New York: Norton.

Sennett, R. (2006) *The Culture of the New Capitalism*. New Haven, CT: Yale University Press.

Sewell, G. and Wilkinson, B. (1992) 'Someone to watch over me: Surveillance, discipline and the just-in-time labour process', *Sociology* 26 (2): 271–89.

Shenhav, Y. (1999) *Manufacturing Rationality*. Oxford: Oxford University Press.

Smircich, L. (1983) 'Concepts of culture and organizational analysis', *Administrative Science Quarterly*, 28: 339–58.

Smith, H. (2011a) 'Greek despair over further cuts sees suicide and crime rates on the rise', *Guardian Online*. Available at http://www.guardian.co.uk/world/2011/sep/24/greek-despair-cuts-suicide-crime. Accessed 24/09/11.

Smith, H. (2011b) 'Greek woes drive up suicide rates', *Guardian Online*. Available at http://www.guardian.co.uk/world/2011/dec/18/greek-woes-suicide-rate-highest. Accessed 30/11/12.

Smyth, C. (2011) 'NHS wastes millions by overpaying for supplies', *The Times*, 3 January, p. 1.

Standing, G. (2011) *The Precariat: The Dangerous New Class*. London: Bloomsbury.

Stark, D. (2009) *The Sense of Dissonance: Accounts of Worth in Economic Life*. Princeton, NJ: Princeton University Press.

Steger, M. and Roy, R. (2010) *Neoliberalism: A Very Short Introduction*. Oxford: Oxford University Press.

Stein, J. (2010) *Pivotal Decade: How the United States Traded Factories for Finance in the 1970s*. Yale University Press.

Stewart, T.A. (1993) 'Reengineering: The hot new managing tool', *Fortune* 128 (4): 32–7.

Strange, S. (1986) *Casino Capitalism*. Oxford: Basil Blackwell.

Strathern, M. (ed.) (1992) *Audit Culture: Anthropological Studies in Accountability, Ethics and the Academy*. London: Routledge.

Tax Justice Network (2011) Available at http://www.taxjustice.net. Accessed 12/12/11.

Tett, G. (2010) *Fool's Gold: How Unrestrained Greed Corrupted a Dream, Shattered Global Markets and Unleashed a Catastrophe*. London: Abacus.

Thomas, R. and Dunkerley, D. (1999) 'Careering downwards? Middle management in the downsized organization', *British Journal of Management* 10 (2): 157–69.

Tienari, J. (2006) 'Critical thinking, no fancy word play [Review of *a very short, fairly interesting and reasonably cheap book about studying organizations* by Chris Grey]', *Organization* 13 (2): 302–3.

Useem, M. (1984) *The Inner Circle: Large Corporations and the Rise of Business Political Activity in the US and UK*. Oxford: Oxford University Press.

Vitali, S., Glattfelder, J.B. and Battiston, S. (2011) 'The network of global corporate control', *PLoS ONE* 6 (10): e25995. doi:10.1371/journal.pone.0025995. Available at http://www.plosone.org/article/info%3Adoi%2F10.1371%2Fjournal.pone.0025995. Accessed 30/12/11.

Voltaire, F. (2001/1759) *Candide*. London: Penguin.

Vroom, V. (1964) *Work and Motivation*. New York: John Wiley.

Warhurst, C. and Thompson, P. (1998) 'Hands, hearts and minds: Changing work and workers at the end of the century', in P. Thompson and C. Warhurst (eds), *Workplaces of the Future*. Basingstoke: Macmillan. pp. 1–24.

Wearden, G. (2010) 'Defend UK firms from foreign takeovers, says former Cadbury boss', *Guardian Online*. Available at http://www.guardian.co.uk/business/2010/feb/09/roger-carr-takeover-rules. Accessed 30/12/11.

Weber, M. (1992/1904–1905) *The Protestant Ethic and the Spirit of Capitalism*. London: Routledge.

Weick, K. (1979) *The Social Psychology of Organizing* New York: McGraw-Hill.

Weil, S. (1949) *L'Enracinement: Prélude á une déclaration des devoirs envers l'être humain*. Paris: Gallimard. [Translated as *The Need for Roots*. New York: Putnam, 1952].

Wheatley, M. (1992) *The Future of Management*. Corby: British Institute of Management.

Whitfield, D. (2011) *PPP Database of Strategic Partnerships 2011*. European Services Strategy Unit. Available at http://www.european-services-strategy.org.uk/news/new-edition-of-ppp-database-on-strategic-partn/ppp-database-2011.pdf. Accessed 18/12/11.

Wilkinson, R. and Pickett, K. (2010) *The Spirit Level: Why Equality is Better for Everyone*. London: Penguin.

Willmott, H. (1993) 'Strength is ignorance, slavery is freedom: Managing culture in modern organizations', *Journal of Management Studies* 30 (4): 515–52.

Wolf, M. (2009) 'Liberalisation sews its own destruction', *Financial Times*, 9 March, p. 13.

Wolfe, T. (1988) *The Bonfire of the Vanities*. London: Jonathan Cape.

Index

Page references to notes will be followed by the letter 'n'